the H●USE of LIFE

BY SHELLEY BRIGGS CALLAHAN

CHOP
SUEY
BOOKS
BOOKS

the H●USE of LIFE

Copyright © 2016 by Shelley Briggs Callahan

All rights reserved.
No part of this book may be reproduced in any form by any electronic or mechanical means including photocopying, recording, or information storage and retrieval without permission in writing from the author.

Published by Chop Suey Books Books
Richmond, VA, USA
chopsueybooks.com

ISBN-10: 0-692-77992-2
ISBN-13: 978-0-692-77992-7

Book Website:
shelleybriggscallahan.com
Author E-mail:
shelleybcallahan@gmail.com

Chapter Illustrations by James Callahan: jamescallahan.co
Cover and book design by Team Eight: teameight.com

Printed in Richmond, VA USA
by Carter Printing Company

for Dick and Barb, of course.

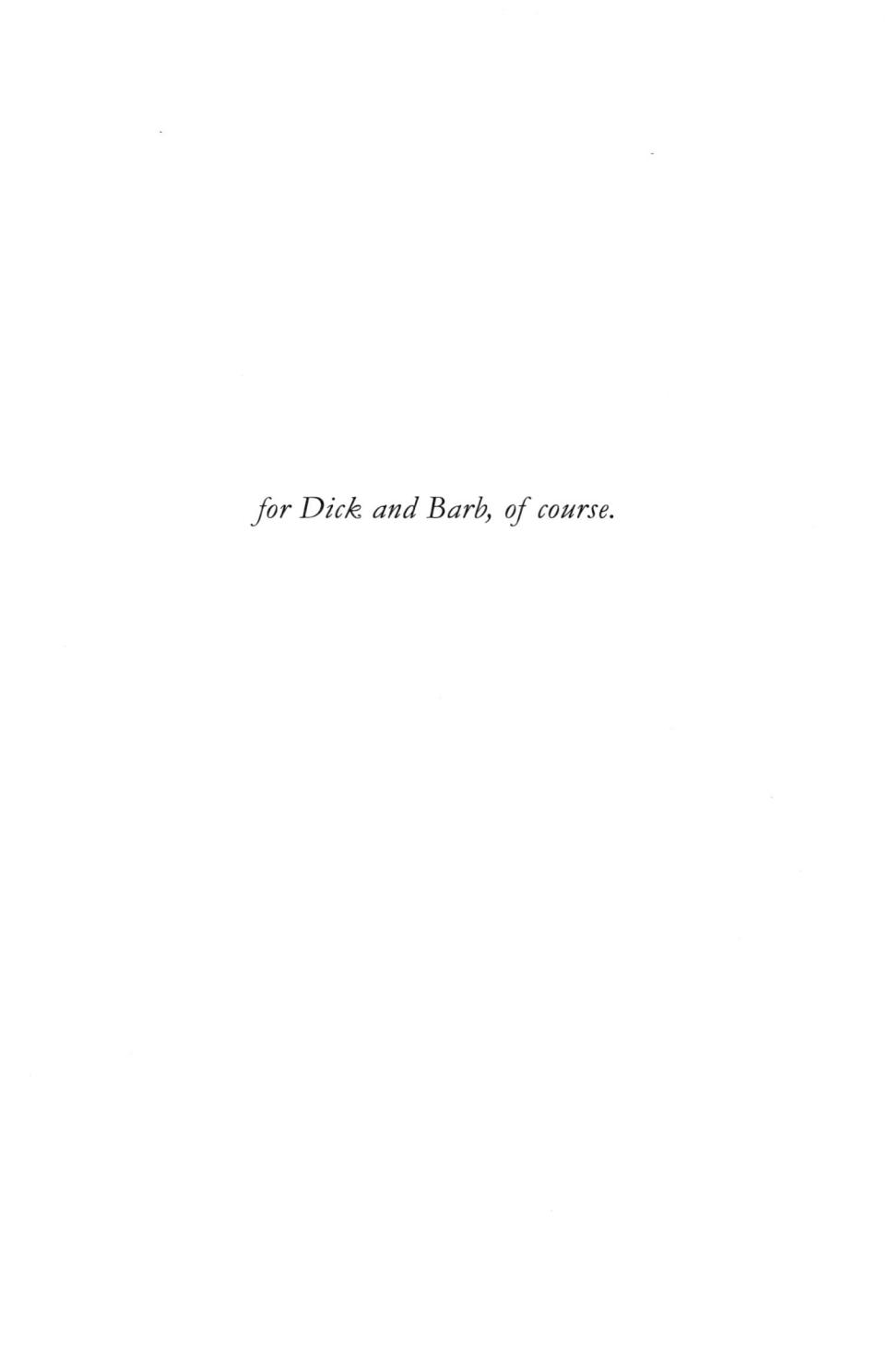

Haiti

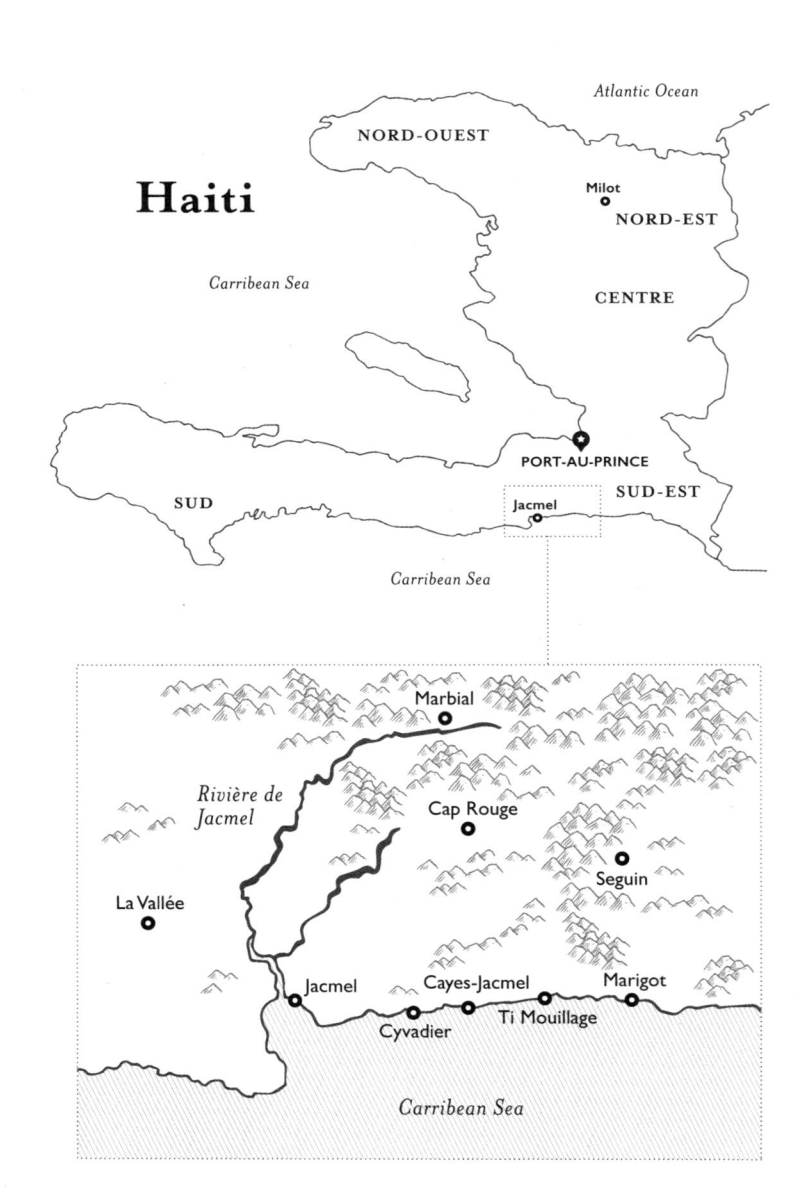

Atlantic Ocean

NORD-OUEST

Milot

NORD-EST

Carribean Sea

CENTRE

PORT-AU-PRINCE

SUD   Jacmel   SUD-EST

Carribean Sea

Marbial

Rivière de Jacmel

Cap Rouge

Seguin

La Vallée

Jacmel   Cayes-Jacmel   Marigot
   Cyvadier   Ti Mouillage

Carribean Sea

Bondye di ou: Fè pa ou, M'a fè Pa M'

"God says to you, you do your part, I will do mine."

HAITIAN PROVERB

INTRODUCTION

Not long after I started recording interviews with Dick and Barb, I knew having enough material to write a book would not be difficult. Between the two, they had an abundance of stories about how they came to build a clinic in Haiti. I told them, without a doubt, the book would write itself. Deciding why I wanted to tell their story was the more difficult part.

This book is about the lives of Dick and Barb Hammond and their work in Haiti for over thirty years. It is a story about their love for the Haitian people. It is about one couple's dedication to helping in a country where the need is great, and change is slow. It is a story about determination, passion, and hope. I knew I wanted to share their story, but I also wanted to be clear about why it was important to tell.

I wanted to give people a reason to believe in Haiti, its people, and its future. I wanted to show how Dick and Barb's path led them to build a clinic in a foreign country—not to present them as having done everything right (for they know that is not the case), but to show how they have always tried to do the most good through persistence, trust, and faith. I wanted people to see that many aid organizations have long, deeply rooted pasts in the countries where they work. Not all organizations only work for a few years and then disappear, leaving behind questions of how money was spent or if anyone actually benefitted—many organizations have worked in Haiti for decades, well before the 2010 earthquake. The founders of these organizations—people like Dick and Barb—have long histories in the country. They have built their homes in Haiti and dedicated their time to helping the Haitian people. These organizations, both small and large, are not leaving—they were there before the earthquake, they stayed after the earthquake, and they will be in Haiti long after their founders are gone.

There are estimated to be between four thousand and ten thousand NGOs currently in Haiti, and each has its own story of how it came to work with the Haitian people. Although they began working in Haiti at different times, these organizations are all there for a reason, and a similar one—to provide for those in need. Why is Dick and Barb's story special, and why does it deserve to be heard? What makes them unique? The answer is simple: their story is special because Dick and Barb are so normal. They are compassionate people who are driven to help others, and nothing much else sets them apart from anyone. They have accomplished a great deal in life, while still remaining personable and modest. They don't claim to know everything or have all the answers. So much of what they have done they have figured out on their own with a great many challenges and obstacles along the way.

Dick and Barb chose to work in a country where it sometimes seems as though change will never come, and that has been so daunting that, at times, they have wanted to leave for good. They have witnessed many tragic circumstances that caused heartbreak day in and day out, yet they still returned, assuring the Haitian people that they were reliable, because there is little to rely on in Haiti. Dick and Barb have never given up hope in their work, because everything they have done has been about giving hope to the Haitian people.

The Hammonds have never received a dime for their efforts. Their dedication and love for the people of Haiti comes from a desire to help those in need, not for monetary gain or for recognition. In many ways, this has kept their organization from

INTRODUCTION

growing, and, at times, (including today) it has made the future of the clinic uncertain. Dick and Barb ask for very little, yet give so much in life. They have built their home in Haiti, and they have opened their doors to thousands upon thousands of people to come inside without hesitation, judgment, or obligation. They are a couple that love each other immensely, as well as those around them. They did their best to tell these stories as accurately as they could—they apologize for any inaccuracies, which are solely due to a lapse in memory because of the passage of time. I am honored to have gotten to spend so much time hearing about their extraordinary lives.

-Shelley Briggs Callahan
May 2016

en

Today was a good day. We saw lots of patients, many of whom were getting better. The most remarkable patient I saw was a woman with diabetes and hypertension. I told my interpreter, Yougains, that her blood sugar was out of control, and her blood pressure was even higher. Although the patient did not speak English, she understood that I was concerned for her, and she started to cry. She was sitting on a short bench, so I moved her bag over, sat down, and put my arm around her.

We talked for a while, and she told me that she had run out of her medications, including those for diabetes. She had gone to the pharmacy in town, but they wanted too much money for the medicine. After listening to her, I worked to get her back on a treatment plan. Afterwards, she said that if it were not for the clinic, she would be dead. What this particular patient said is in fact correct—so many patients would not ever be treated if it were not for the clinic, and they would never receive medication.

This woman made the whole trip to Haiti worthwhile. The clinic is about the patients, and we are making a big difference.

By the way, the Haitians call this place "The House of Life."

-Bill, MD
September 2014

CHAPTER 1: EN

Just the day before, Dick and Barb Hammond had been at the Hotel Montana in Port-au-Prince having lunch. As usual, Boyer, a Haitian man who worked for Dick, had driven in from Jacmel to pick them up from the Toussaint Louverture International Airport. Along with Dick and Barb on the trip was their longtime friend Larry, who they knew from back home. After their plane landed and they retrieved their bags, they met Boyer outside the airport. They loaded their luggage into the back of the pick-up truck and headed to the hotel to eat, and relax, before driving to the clinic near Jacmel, a few hours south of Port-au-Prince.

The Hotel Montana is a well-known landmark in Pétionville, a suburb of Port-au-Prince. Located in the rolling hills of the city, the hotel is famous for hosting journalists and reporters from around the world, offering a stunning panoramic view of the city from the pool terrace. Dick and Barb had often met interesting travelers at the Hotel Montana—aid workers, contractors, vacationers. Once, they met a few men who had flown to Haiti to search for gold. They regularly made stops to dine or stay the night at the hotel as they traveled in and out of Port-au-Prince, sometimes as many as eight times a year.

After lunch, they headed to the Caribbean Market, a local grocery store that, with its aisles of packaged food and refrigerated items, was much more typical of an American supermarket than most stores in Haiti. Barb dove into her shopping list, having meticulously planned out meals for the upcoming weeks—the visiting medical team, consisting of upwards of twenty-five people, would be arriving at the clinic soon, and getting all the necessary items took a great deal of preparation. Since the Caribbean Market offered more options than the smaller markets near the clinic, it was important for Barb to get everything she needed while they were in Port-au-

Prince—the drive from Jacmel to Port-au-Prince took anywhere from three to five hours depending on traffic, and there would not be time to make the trip back for missing supplies. After the shopping was done, the group loaded the groceries into the back of the truck and headed out of the capital towards Jacmel. The clinic, Dick and Barb's second home, awaited, empty since the last time they were in Haiti.

The next day, Tuesday, January 12, 2010, at 16:53 local time, both the Hotel Montana and the Caribbean Market would collapse, completely devastated by the 7.0 magnitude earthquake that would rattle the country, the epicenter only twenty-five kilometers west of Port-au-Prince.

*

When the earthquake struck, Dick and Barb were standing in the grass behind the clinic visiting with Diolene, a young Haitian woman who worked in the clinic pharmacy. Diolene was one of the clinic workers Dick and Barb saw with regularity—most of the others they saw only when the clinic was operating. When Dick and Barb were in Haiti, Diolene usually came by on Sundays to accompany them to church. When the clinic was in session, she worked each day in the pharmacy to help the volunteer medical team seeing Haitian patients. On this particular Monday, Diolene had come by to welcome the Hammonds back. She had not seen them since the last clinic, the previous November, and with eight weeks in between clinics, she was anxious to greet them. Like many of the Haitian staff, Diolene was close to the couple, affectionately referring to them as "Mom" and "Dad."

As they stood chatting, Dick and Barb talked about their plans to stay at the clinic until March. It would be a shorter trip for them, lasting only about two months—even in their early

CHAPTER 1: EN

seventies, it wasn't unusual for Dick and Barb to spend more than half the year in Haiti.

Without warning, the ground began to shake.

"What's happening?" Barb screamed.

"It's an earthquake!" Dick yelled back.

Barb and Diolene grabbed onto Dick to keep from falling. As they tried to remain standing on unbalanced ground, Barb watched as the cement pillars of the clinic swayed, something she knew was not supposed to happen. For thirty seconds—thirty very long seconds—they stood as still as possible, holding onto one another, waiting for the earth to calm.

The only person inside the clinic at the time of the earthquake was Larry. He had just turned off the clinic's computer, located on the top floor of the building, and was walking down the stairs, when he paused on the landing between the second and third floor. There on the landing, he heard a noise that sounded like a train on the roof. He rushed down the stairs to the kitchen and saw the cupboard doors opening and closing. Dried goods and dishes were falling out, crashing to the floor. He looked back up the stairs and saw the computer tumble off the desk, landing right next to where he had just been seated. It was then that he realized what he was experiencing was an earthquake, and the train sound was the earth grinding against itself. Larry ran down the stairs and stood in a doorway between the kitchen and the men's dorm-style bedroom.

As soon as the ground quieted, Dick looked up toward the three-story clinic.

"Larry, where are you? Are you OK?" he yelled.

"Yeah, Dick, I'm fine," Larry shouted down from the kitchen.

Larry hurried down the stairs and outside to where Dick, Barb, and Diolene were standing. He told them the computer had broken to pieces and the kitchen was a mess. Otherwise, he was uninjured, and, as far as he could tell, not much other damage had been sustained inside the clinic.

From where they were standing, they couldn't tell how much harm had been done to the structure of the building—the clinic, however, had not collapsed, and that was relieving. But it wasn't the clinic Dick was worried about. He didn't know the magnitude of the earthquake at that moment, but he knew it had to have caused considerable destruction. The only thing he could think about was how fragile the lives of Haitians were already without a natural disaster occurring.

Dick, Barb, and Larry walked around the side of the clinic to the driveway, surveying the damage. Just as they turned the corner, they saw Boyer flying through the gate, the truck bouncing down the rocky, uneven path. He was on his way back to the clinic when the earthquake struck. He had been visiting his friend, Big Louie, who lived a short distance down the road. The group waved at Boyer so he could see they were outside and safe. When he stopped the truck just short of Dick and Barb, his eyes were as big as saucers. He didn't know if the clinic would be standing, or if anyone had been inside, and he was obviously shaken.

For a few minutes, they all stood together and tried to calm down. Once ready to focus, Boyer and Dick began circling the building, checking out the foundation and the walls of the clinic. To their relief, they found that damages outside the clinic were minimal—they saw a number of hairline cracks, but the building itself was intact. Dick and Barb were incredibly grateful. They were fortunate to have built a structure strong enough to withstand such a massive quake. But, they were about to find out just how catastrophic the earthquake had been—not far from the

CHAPTER 1: EN

clinic property, Jacmel was devastated.

*

When his house started shaking, Dr. Frantzso Nelson did not know what was happening. He had never experienced an earthquake before. For years after, what he would remember most would be the noise, not just of the earthquake itself, but the sounds coming from the street after the ground stopped shaking—the cries and screams that rang out in every direction.

Dr. Nelson, who simply goes by Nelson to those who know him, is a Haitian doctor who has known Dick and Barb since 2007. The surgical and medical liaison for the clinic, he also has his own medical practice at the Dr. Martinez Hospital in Jacmel. At the time of the earthquake, he was nearing the completion of a two-story home in town that had been under construction for a few years. He, his wife, Anne, and their daughter, Caedelina, were on the second floor of the house during the quake. Anne was pregnant at the time.

When the earthquake ended, and the house stopped shaking and creaking, Nelson and his family crept downstairs and walked out onto the street. All around their home, other houses and buildings had collapsed into rubble—dust clouds fogged their view. Although Nelson and his family were unharmed, as he looked around, he saw people everywhere in the road bleeding, covered in concrete powder. He knew he needed to get to the hospital as soon as possible—there he would have medical supplies to help the injured. A neighbor close by offered to take care of Nelson's wife and their daughter. Knowing his family was in good hands, he hurried towards the Dr. Martinez Hospital on foot.

By the time Nelson arrived shortly after, dozens of people

had already gathered outside the hospital, many of them in desperate need of medical attention. Several of them were praying and calling out to God. The bodies of those who had managed to walk to the hospital, only to die in front of the hospital's doors, lay in the street.

From outside, Nelson could tell the building was not badly damaged—he could see a few cracks along the walls and some concrete blocks that had broken off, but it appeared safe to enter. He hurried inside and started the hospital's small generator, restoring the electricity he would need to care for patients.

He then began bringing in people one by one. Not too long after Nelson started treating the wounded, Dr. Martinez, the owner of the hospital, appeared with two other physicians. The four doctors worked as fast as they could to help those who had lost limbs, those with head wounds, and those who were bleeding profusely. The number of people in need far exceeded their resources and the space available in the hospital, but they continued to work tirelessly, desperately trying to save lives.

They did not stop working until the following morning at 5:00, when the generator ran out of gas. They could no longer power the hospital's equipment, and their medical supplies were depleted. They had no choice but to say "no more." Nelson would remain haunted by the memory of people dying inside the operating room, waiting for blood transfusions that the hospital was unable to provide.

Exhausted, Nelson returned home to check on his wife and daughter and to see the condition of his house. He had left in such a hurry the day before, he was not entirely sure how much damage had been caused. When he arrived, he found his new home in shambles, having collapsed on itself in the aftershocks of the earthquake.

CHAPTER 1: EN

*

Nelson slept in a courtyard outside of his house that evening, as Anne and Caedelina continued to stay with a neighbor. The next night, after working all day at the hospital, he slept outside again, along with thousands of other Haitians in Jacmel whose homes had been destroyed. A few days later, aid organizations started to arrive in town and hand out tents. Tent communities began popping up everywhere, and they were expansive—well beyond the number of people who had lost their homes. Many of the Haitians who had houses to return to still preferred to stay in tents because they were terrified of another earthquake. For years to come, many people in Haiti wouldn't feel comfortable sleeping inside.

The first night Nelson tried to sleep in his tent, he restlessly tossed and turned, as aftershocks continued to shake Jacmel. But the aftershocks weren't what kept him awake. He was worried about his daughter and wife, and their unborn child. He laid there questioning how he was going to keep them safe among all the wreckage and chaos in Jacmel. Nelson knew he had to keep working in the hospital every day, all day long—too many Haitians were in need of a doctor.

Fortunately, he didn't have to wait long for an answer. Within a few days, as more and more aid organizations moved into Jacmel, a representative from the French Embassy in Haiti approached him. The embassy was evacuating as many people as they could to France, temporarily, and the representative wanted to get Nelson and his family on a plane as soon as possible. Nelson told the representative that he wanted Anne and Caedelina to go—however, he would stay in Jacmel and continue working. Jacmel was his hometown, and it was out of the question to abandon his people at a time like this. It was agreed his wife and daughter would go without him, and they left almost immediately. Content knowing his family was out of harm's way, Nelson got back to work without worry.

That night, after another exhausting day at the hospital, Nelson once again went to sleep in his tent. But his peace wasn't to last. At 4:00 a.m. he was jolted awake by loud snoring right next to him. A man had moved into his tent, which was barely big enough for Nelson alone, and had fallen asleep.

Nelson jumped up and yelled, "Outside! Outside!" as he began pulling the man by his feet.

The man reluctantly got up and left the tent, but Nelson couldn't sleep after the incident. He went back to the hospital instead. He told himself if he couldn't go home, he would stay at work. He was fed up with trying to sleep outdoors.

The next day, a woman came to the hospital, complaining to Nelson about bad pains in her back. When he asked her if she knew why she was having the pains, she told him it was from sleeping outside. She did not have a tent, and she was sleeping on the ground.

Nelson responded, his eyes growing wide, "OK ma'am! I know of a tent that you can have right away."

*

Dick and Barb slept inside the clinic, in their own bed, the night of the earthquake, much to the dismay of many Haitians. But they were not as worried about the aftershocks or another earthquake occurring. They were concerned about not being able to get in touch with family at home. They had had no luck with phone calls going through to the United States the day of the earthquake, so they had not communicated with anyone, and they

CHAPTER 1: EN

knew their children must be worried about them. Dick and Barb had also gotten word that regularly scheduled flights to Haiti were all canceled, meaning the medical team was going to have to make alternate arrangements to get into the country. Toussaint Louverture International Airport was badly damaged, and flights were restricted to US military supply planes and aid groups only. It was imperative to get in touch with the team to make sure they were still going to make it to the clinic.

When they woke up the morning after the earthquake, Dick was able to reach his son Martin on the phone first. He assured Martin the clinic was fine and ready to function just as soon as the team could get to Haiti. After they hung up, Martin made calls to the team members, who busily worked to find alternative means to fly. Dick and Barb waited anxiously. It was a real possibility that the team would not make it to Haiti at all, and that made them extremely nervous.

The clinic hosts six medical teams a year, around the same time each January, March, May, July, September, and November. The teams are made up of doctors, nurses, and other trained medical professionals, as well as non-medical volunteers, who work together for a two-week period to see as many Haitian patients as time and resources permit. Considering the magnitude of the earthquake, Dick and Barb desperately needed the team to get to the clinic that January—and quickly. The Haitian people relied on the medical teams, and, after such a devastating disaster, their presence would be more important than ever.

Almost a week would go by before Dick and Barb got word that the team was definitely going to make it into Haiti. Fortunately, given their backgrounds, a few of the medical volunteers had great resources when it came to disaster relief response, and they were able to make connections with private companies to fly them into the country. Some of the team members would be flying in small planes with other disaster relief workers, and some would be finding single seats on flights that were carrying in aid. Dick and Barb were so thankful. Though the makeup of the team had changed because of the earthquake—some of the volunteers originally scheduled to go to Haiti had to back out, and some new volunteers jumped in last minute—in the end, a full team of roughly twenty volunteers had committed.

During regular clinics, the volunteers flew into Miami from various locations across the United States to convene before flying to Port-au-Prince as a group. They would then take a short flight (or make the drive from Port-au-Prince) to the clinic in Jacmel. This time, because of the earthquake, the team would have to be rerouted to fly into Ft. Lauderdale Executive Airport where various private planes would bring them straight into the Jacmel airport, about seven miles away from the clinic, skipping over Port-au-Prince entirely. Since the team members would be flying separately, it would take longer to get them into the country, but considering the circumstances, Dick and Barb felt lucky the team was going to make it to Haiti at all.

*

The day after the earthquake, Boyer drove Dick, Barb, and Larry into Jacmel to see the damage. None of them had ever seen so much wreckage and devastation. The town had been reduced to piles of broken-up concrete, which blocked the sidewalks and the streets. Power lines were down everywhere they looked. Outside of the St. Michel Hospital, the main hospital in Jacmel, the scene was gruesome—family members stood weeping, closely protecting the bodies of their loved ones who

CHAPTER 1: EN

lay dead in the street. Some yelled out for help that was nowhere to be found—aid workers had yet to arrive in Jacmel.

Boyer drove the group to the Department of Health, located near the center of town. The building, which Dick had visited dozens of times since he began working in Haiti, was now only recognizable by its sign. Before the earthquake, the sign had hung at the top of the three-story building, but now, as Dick stood next to the collapsed structure, the same sign, still attached to the crushed concrete, hung at shoulder level.

As they continued to walk through the streets of Jacmel, everyone they saw was in shock. They stopped and talked to a few local Haitians, and their reactions were all the same—no one could begin to think how Haiti would ever recover from such a horrible disaster. Before they returned to the truck to drive back to the clinic, the group noticed a few Haitian men sitting at a table in the middle of the street. One of the men was shuffling a deck of cards. The others were silent as they waited for the dealer to deal the next hand. Dick and Barb watched as the men sat and played their card game while the world around them was in ruins. There was nothing else these men could do. No one could do anything. There was no electricity, no water, no food, no medical aid, no emergency relief. No one could start to repair the damage. Everything was dead. There was nothing to do but sit and wait for help to arrive.

*

By the second day after the earthquake, aid organizations started appearing in Jacmel. The first foreign response teams were Canadian, followed closely by the Americans. And it was not just a few aid organizations—Dick estimates that maybe thirty or more international groups showed up in rapid succession. As relief workers poured in, the mayor and his entourage attempted to organize the groups around the center of town, but the situation was chaotic. The physicians who arrived with supplies set up tents and tables, and started treating the injured. Other physicians, however, had arrived with no medical supplies or medications, giving them no way to treat patients. So many groups had entered Jacmel all at once that it was almost impossible to organize all of them. Although the number of relief workers arriving in Jacmel showed Haitians how much foreigners were willing to support them, it was difficult to tell what was going on, not only for the aid organizations, but for the Haitians as well.

It would still be a few days before the clinic's medical team would start landing in Jacmel, so while they waited, Dick and Boyer made trips to and from the Jacmel airport to pick up supplies. Just as the aid organizations had arrived rapidly and in large numbers, so too had the supplies to the airport. The airport personnel were not prepared for the heavy traffic. No one person was responsible for aid coming into the warehouse and no one was in control of how supplies were being dealt out. No one seemed to know which supplies belonged to which organization. Dick would receive a manifest with his name on it, and, after picking up the boxes and bringing them back to the clinic, he would find they weren't medical supplies at all. He tried to return one such shipment. After receiving boxes containing items that were of no use to him, Dick had Boyer drive them back to the airport. But the Customs Department refused to accept the boxes. They didn't know what to do with the returned supplies— no one had ever brought anything *back* to the airport.

A few days after the earthquake, authorities with the Department of Health asked Dick if he would consider bringing

CHAPTER 1: EN

the medical team into town once they arrived so they could work closer to the patients living in the more severely damaged areas, instead of having the Haitians make the trip to the clinic. The clinic was located in a sector just outside Jacmel known as Cyvadier, about an hour by foot from the center of town, or a fifteen-minute drive. Cyvadier was not as populated as Jacmel, nor was it as badly affected by the disaster. The thought was that if Dick brought the team, along with medical supplies, to Jacmel to work side-by-side with the other aid organizations, the team might be able to help more patients than they otherwise would.

Dick contemplated the idea of working outside of the clinic. He knew they could pull it off—for fifteen years, the medical teams had operated without a permanent home, using various buildings near Jacmel to treat patients. But even though Dick knew it was possible, it wouldn't allow for the most ideal conditions—the team would have to move supplies and medications, water and food, as well as create makeshift exam tables and privacy tents. At the clinic, everything would be accessible and familiar for the team, many of whom were returning volunteers.

After serious consideration, Dick declined the mayor's request. The volunteers would work more efficiently if they stayed at the clinic as planned, and he did not want to disturb the clinic's already established system, both as a benefit to the patients and to the medical team. Dick was also worried that with so many other aid organizations already in Jacmel, he would only be adding to the disorder. He did, however, assure the Department of Health authorities that *any* Haitian patient that came to the clinic would be taken care of to the best of the medical team's ability. But, this was no different than it had been before the earthquake—anyone was welcome to visit the clinic for care, no matter the circumstances. Haitians in Jacmel, as well as around the entire country, knew that they could rely on the Friends of the Children of Haiti clinic.

*

The Friends of the Children of Haiti medical clinic, more commonly referred to as the FOTCOH clinic, is an impressive building. The 6,000-square-foot facility is made entirely of concrete, all painted freshly white, and is designed to comfortably host up to twenty-five visiting volunteers at a time. Each year, nearly 150 volunteers work at the clinic, serving over 15,000 Haitian patients.

The clinic is divided between three floors. The top floor houses Dick and Barb's private room. The couple usually spends more than six months out of the year in Haiti, and the clinic serves as their second home. Two additional small bedrooms are located on the third floor, along with two desks. One desk is for the clinic computer, and one is for Dick's endless paperwork—payroll stubs, receipts, invoices, clinic schedules, and patient reports. A balcony surrounds three sides of the top floor, offering a gorgeous view of the Caribbean Sea, as well as the plush landscape of the clinic property. Most nights, volunteers spend their time sitting on the balcony, shuffling plastic patio chairs to accommodate a preferred view, whether facing west, south, or east. Looking out over the ocean, only a few lights flicker off the coast, and the tranquility one finds serves as a perfect reset after a long day of work.

The kitchen is located on the clinic's second floor. Plastic tables and wooden chairs fill the large room. Barb is usually in the kitchen, along with a few Haitian staff members, preparing meals for volunteers. Their work begins at 5:30 a.m., before the

CHAPTER 1: EN

sun comes up, and goes well into the afternoon. During the day, when the team isn't gathered together to eat, the tables are used to count pills for the pharmacy, to fold laundry, or for Dick and Barb to organize piles of dossiers, a French term used to refer to a patient's record. At night, the team can be found in the kitchen playing games or cards, or working on puzzles. A larger balcony is attached to the second floor off the kitchen, providing enough room for the whole team to gather for socializing. The remainder of the second floor is occupied by the men and women's dorm-style rooms, which are large enough to accommodate beds for all the volunteers and provide storage for personal belongings.

The first floor of the building is dedicated entirely to the medical clinic, though most patients won't enter the building, except to visit the pharmacy. Each morning, the clinic's Haitian staff sets up plastic tables and chairs outside the building. Directly out front, certain tables are designated for triaging patients. Once done with triage, patients are sent to a separate area to be seen by a doctor, whose tables are set up on the carport, underneath the second-floor balcony. Then, if needed, a patient is sent inside either for examination in a private exam room, to receive wound care or to visit the lab for testing. Dental patients and gynecological patients are seen inside the clinic as well, in separately marked rooms. Storage rooms on the first floor are filled with medications and medical supplies. The pharmacy also has a small waiting area, where patients receive instructions on how to take their medications properly.

The FOTCOH clinic is widely known in Jacmel, and the locals know of Dick and Barb Hammond, whether they have ever met them or not, because of their long history working in Haiti. Haitians regard the clinic with the utmost respect, wearing their best clothes when visiting. Each team's arrival to the clinic is greatly anticipated by the community. Haitians patiently stand in line for hours outside the clinic walls, sometimes even sleeping overnight. Some Haitians walk for days to be seen by the medical volunteers. The clinic provides consistent care that so many Haitians lack, and for most of them, the clinic is the only option they have to receive medical treatment. In Haiti, the clinic is a symbol of hope, and of life.

*

I met Dick and Barb in November of 2011, on my first trip to Haiti. In May of the same year, my sister Erin traveled to the clinic to volunteer. When she returned home, she had wonderful stories to tell about her experience. She excitedly talked about all the people she had met and how much she felt like a part of the team, even as a first-time volunteer.

A pharmacist, Erin had initially read about FOTCOH in a pharmacy magazine that described the work of the organization. At the time Erin came across the article, Dick and Barb had already been working in Haiti for nearly twenty-five years. Erin was impressed by the article and, having been looking for a volunteer opportunity, signed up. She volunteered with FOTCOH without knowing much more than what she had read, but she enjoyed her time at the clinic working alongside the other volunteers and the Haitian staff so much so that she continued to return to Haiti year after year. Soon, she had recruited me and other friends to volunteer along with her, and we have all returned numerous times.

FOTCOH's dedicated volunteer group is unyielding—over the years, hundreds of people from all over the United States have taken time away from their jobs and families, spending their own money to travel to Haiti so they can work at the clinic. The

CHAPTER 1: EN

volunteers are like family to one another, looking forward to seeing each other once or twice a year, like children do at summer camp. Special relationships develop in a few short weeks, which is not surprising. It is hard to not become closely knit—the team works, eats, sleeps, and relaxes in the same building. Daily activities are done in groups, not only to ensure the safety of the volunteers, but also to give everyone an opportunity to bond, because, outside of Haiti, many of the team members would not have crossed paths in their lives.

Dick and Barb value the volunteers immensely, and it shows in everything they do. They are incredibly welcoming, starting from the first moment the team gets to the clinic, preparing beds and food ahead of time to make everyone feel at home. They are genuinely concerned about every volunteer, and they take the time to ask them questions and get to know the team the best they can. But Dick and Barb's appreciation is shown most greatly by their sheer presence in Haiti—they attend every clinic possible, even when it is suggested by doctors or others that they not do so. And that was what stood out in Erin's mind on her first trip. She was blown away when she stepped off the plane in Jacmel and the *founders* of the organization were standing on the runway.

Along with personally greeting every team that they can, Dick and Barb also work alongside the volunteers each day, having their own responsibilities at the clinic. And they are no spring chickens—both Dick and Barb were already in their mid-seventies in 2011 when I met them. But they rarely seemed phased by the oppressive heat in Haiti or by how much work it takes to run the clinic. As rewarding as the work is, it is also exhausting, yet they rarely let it show. Neither of them moves around quickly, and Dick grumbles about how tired he is often, as though he is mad at his body, but he does more than many people half his age. I frequently think of Dick puttering up and down the stairs at the clinic, taking every chance he gets to remind me how he used to run up the stairs like I can. But even as a 31-year-old in good health, I am baffled by how much energy Dick and Barb have. And then I remember, Dick was twice as old as I was when I met him when he started building the clinic in Haiti.

For me, getting to know Dick and Barb has been one of the most enjoyable aspects of volunteering at the clinic. Dick is serious, without a doubt, but has a great sense of humor, and he is one of the best storytellers I have ever met, as well as a great listener. He has a stern, intimidating face that can easily transform into a full grin when he finds something humorous, which is often. At one moment, he might blow his top at something that has frustrated him (and he will yell if he feels it is warranted), and the next moment he gets teary-eyed when discussing the future of the clinic and what might become of it after he is gone. He is not erratic for these reasons—he is raw and heartfelt, and he cares intensely about others. Though it may sometimes seem as though Dick doesn't know what is going on around the clinic, this is never the case. He is quietly observing the team, wondering if they are having a good time, or if the work is too much for anyone. He is also incredibly in tune with the needs of the Haitian patients and staff, as is Barb, and for that they are loved dearly in Haiti, and they love the Haitian people just as strongly.

But to truly describe Dick Hammond, you have to talk about Dick and Barb together. They are not separate as people, although they have distinctly different personalities. Barb is more relaxed, giggling to herself as she works her way around

CHAPTER 1: EN

the kitchen. She is small and feisty, and she never seems to stop moving, unless she is working on a puzzle or playing a game, and then her hands move just as fast as her mind does. Barb seems to find humor in almost everything, and she takes care of volunteers and Haitians alike in a way that is motherly and comforting. As I began to learn how well Dick and Barb complemented each other, it came to light how they managed to build a clinic in Haiti—they do everything together and are partners in all their endeavors—even apart, they rarely make decisions without consulting one another.

Something that has always impressed me about Dick and Barb, besides their determination and drive, is the fact that they started working in Haiti well past their youth, and even past middle age. When most people would be settling into retirement, Dick and Barb were just getting started on their life's work.

de

I have been blessed to come to Haiti with FOTCOH six times now as a non-medical volunteer. I have been especially blessed to have a daughter of mine come with me for the first time on this trip. I love experiencing what has become routine for me through eyes that are experiencing Haiti, and the clinic, for the first time.

While the overall operation of the clinic has become routine, every day brings new people and situations. I am privileged to work with the crowd assessing patients before they enter the clinic. Some of the patients have become familiar to me, as I now remember their faces and sometimes even their names. I am sad when we hear of a patient whose case seems hopeless, and rejoice when a patient's health improves.

On one of the first days at clinic, we saw a child who was only a month old and underweight and malnourished. The physician who saw the child sent baby formula home with the mother, and told her to bring him back in a few days, on the upcoming Saturday. The physician later told the team that the baby very likely would not live until then. When I went out into the crowd on Saturday morning, the mother and child were not there. I cried, because that meant that the child had probably died. Later, as we were winding up for the day, I looked up, and there was mom and baby! I cried again, this time thanking God for this tiny child that was fighting to survive. His chances are still not good, but I'll continue to pray for this little guy, and I am hoping to see him at clinic in November.

-Ken, Non-Medical Volunteer
May 2015

CHAPTER 2: DE

What Barb would remember most about the first time she stepped foot in Haiti was the smell.

The Hammonds had just walked off a ship in Port-au-Prince when they were greeted by a Haitian tour guide. They were on a ten-day cruise through the Caribbean, and their boat would be docked in the city's harbor for the afternoon. Dick and Barb had arranged for a tour, hoping to take in the local culture. The guide shuffled the couple away from the port into the busy streets. They both noticed immediately that Port-au-Prince was littered with garbage, and the crowds were immense—the press of humanity was stifling.

They arrived at their destination, a massive iron and metal building only a few blocks from the ocean. A large clock tower faced them, high above the entranceway of the building and the crowded street below, beyond which ran two long hallways. It was clear the structure had suffered badly from years of neglect and weather damage. Despite its dreary appearance, the building was still filled with bustling Haitians coming and going in all directions. The smell hit Barb immediately. The scent of sweat, rotten meat, and burnt coal enveloped them. The air felt heavy, as if they were walking through fog.

Outside the building, dilapidated wooden tables and worn-out blankets filled the sidewalk and spilled into the street, making the road impassable by car. Corn, cabbage, potatoes, grains, coal, shoes, and clothes were piled high off the ground. Women standing in the road pulled items out of baskets perched upon their heads, while others kept their goods in wooden carts. Fish and raw vegetables lay on top of tarps, covered in flies in the baking sun. The heat was strong and consuming.

The guide led Dick and Barb inside the building, threading his way through wall-to-wall people, down aisles so narrow they had to turn sideways to pass. Dick and Barb followed closely, not understanding where they were being led. The guide dodged mangy dogs in the aisles and ducked under endless rows of hanging dresses and pants. Dick and Barb didn't know where to turn. There didn't seem to be any organization to the place. So much was packed into the building it was astounding—a labyrinth of cheap household products, crafts, spices, herbs, perfumes, and beauty products. Meat hung from hooks suspended from the rafters—below the meat dangled the severed head of the animal to which it had been attached. Haitians stopped the couple, grabbed their hands, and shoved bracelets or canvas paintings toward them, trying to make a sale, while speaking in rapid Creole. It didn't matter what they were saying—Dick and Barb couldn't understand. They didn't know the language.

They were being guided through the Marché en Fer, or the Iron Market. Located in the main commercial district of Port-au-Prince, Haiti's capital, the Iron Market was packed daily with merchants ready to sell anything they could to try to make a living. The building had never been properly maintained, which just added to the misery of the whole scene—a decaying structure with thousands upon thousands of Haitians milling about, trying desperately to make a meager income. For many people, the market was their only chance at a livelihood.

The options for work in Haiti are sparse at best. In a country greatly affected by political turmoil, poverty, and lack of infrastructure, Haitians have few choices when it comes to employment. The unemployment rate in Haiti is over forty percent, and more than half of Haitians live in extreme poverty, trying to survive on less than one US dollar a day. Haitian women mostly work in the markets in an effort to support their families.

CHAPTER 2: DE

Haitian men try to find work as farmers or construction workers, or, if they have transportation, they work as tap tap drivers, the Haitian term for a taxicab. Unfortunately, these jobs offer little security, are often dangerous, and require frequent travel away from home and family.

Dick and Barb didn't consider any part of their tour fulfilling. In fact, the port stop in Port-au-Prince was nauseating for them both. Although seeing how Haitians made paintings and woodcarvings had been interesting, the poverty in Port-au-Prince was like nothing they had ever experienced, and it left them with a sour feeling so unpleasant that they wanted to get out as soon as they could.

It was 1974. The Hammonds had just seen Haiti for the first time. They knew instantly that they never wanted to go back.

*

Richard "Dick" Hammond and Barbara "Barb" Rothan both grew up in the 1940s and 1950s in and around Peoria, Illinois. Barb considered her childhood to be privileged. She was raised in a solid, loving family, who, although not wealthy, had most things that money could buy. Education was important to Barb's parents, as well as faith and dedication to family. Barb's parents set an example for her by taking care of their own parents when they were older, and she grew up with a strong consideration for helping others. By the standards for the time in America, Dick's family was middle class. Although they weren't wealthy, they had what they needed—a house, a car, and food on the table. Growing up, Dick remembered being aware of other children who didn't have anything at home, and it was especially apparent to him around the holidays. He knew of families that didn't have Christmas at all, and that stuck with him throughout his life.

Dick and Barb both grew up in the Catholic Church. The couple met for the first time in high school, when Dick showed up unexpectedly to a Halloween party at Barb's house—he had only been invited at the last minute to even out the number of girls and boys after another boy had backed out. They married on August 17, 1957. Not long after, Barb's father helped them secure money from the bank so they could build a house in Bartonville, a suburb of Peoria.

Dick and Barb both attended Bradley University in Peoria. Barb received her Masters of Education, and went on to become a first grade school teacher, a role she continued in for thirty-seven years. When Dick finished school, not many jobs were available. At the time, Dick's father worked at Caterpillar, a major manufacturer of construction and mining equipment in Peoria. He offered to get Dick a job, but Dick declined. He had listened to his father talk about his job, and even though he knew it was an important one, Dick knew it wasn't for him. He was worried he would turn out to be nothing more than a number within a large company like that, and he wanted more freedom with his work.

Instead, Dick accepted an offer to work part-time at an architectural woodworking facility, the George J. Rothan Company, which was owned by Barb's father and her uncle, George Rothan Sr. The job was meant to be temporary, a means for Dick to get his bearings in the workforce. Temporary ended up lasting a long time—forty-five years to be exact. Dick eventually became partner of the company, along with Barb's cousin, George Rothan Jr. When George and Dick took over the company, most of their clients were local, and the bulk of their business was providing millwork for residential constructions. They both worked hard to grow the business and expand their work nationwide. Eventually the company exclusively worked on large commercial buildings—projects such as courthouses, libraries, and colleges and universities. Two of Dick's most memorable jobs were a college library in Oakland, California, and a college library in Connecticut. The work was very rewarding for Dick, and he was proud of all the company's accomplishments.

Even before Dick and Barb were married, they knew they wanted to have a large family. After four years of trying to get pregnant with no success, adoption became the right option to fulfill their dream. Although they didn't have in mind a certain number of children to adopt, they had always been impressed by stories of couples that took in numerous children. They were eager to start the process, because adopting meant that they would not only have a family of their own, but that they could also help children who were without a permanent home. They applied through a local adoption agency and anxiously waited to hear back, even after being told they could expect it to take up to two years before a child was available.

But before the adoption agency had a chance to pair them with an adopted child, Dick and Barb brought home a foster child. It was 1961, and the young boy, William, was a student in Barb's special education class. When it came to her attention that his foster family was no longer able to take care of him, Barb asked Dick if they could take William in so he wouldn't end up back in the foster care system. Dick agreed it was the right thing to do, and they decided, if approved, they would take over as William's foster parents. William was eight years old when the state decided he would move into the Hammonds' household.

In 1963, Dick and Barb got their first call from the adoption agency, nearly two years after applying, just as they had been told. They brought home Michelle, a small baby girl, and the second child in their family. Not long after, to their surprise, the agency had another child available for adoption, if they were ready. They felt prepared to take in another child, and they adopted a little boy named Matthew. Then, shortly after Matthew came to live with them, they got another call—a girl, Melissa, was in need of a home. All three children were under a year old when they were adopted. They had come into Dick and Barb's lives so quickly, people would ask Barb which of the children were the twins, to which she would reply, "Your pick!"

Dick and Barb did not believe pregnancy was possible, so when Barb became pregnant with Martin in 1975, eighteen years after the couple was married, he was a surprise to the whole family. Barb was thirty-nine years old. Michelle, Matthew, and Melissa were in their early teens—William was already out of high school and working. The family was thrilled. Martin's addition to their lives was a pleasure for them all.

For four years in the late 1970s, while raising their children at home, Dick and Barb also sponsored a refugee family from Vietnam, who had been relocated to Peoria due to political unrest. The family was large—a father, a mother, five children, and two grandchildren all arrived in the United States together. Dick and Barb owned a house they used as a rental property that was vacant at the time, so the family lived there. Barb arranged for doctor's visits and helped the father and older daughter search for employment. The two found jobs in Peoria, and the younger children and grandchildren attended local schools. Barb taught the family English, and they became independent quickly, which Dick and Barb were proud of. The two families developed a close relationship, having dinner together on occasion—Dick and Barb were even honored guests at one of their daughter's weddings.

CHAPTER 2: DE

Dick and Barb loved traveling as a family to show the children as much of the country as they could. They even found themselves repeating some of their vacations as the years went on, since Martin had arrived so much later than his siblings and they didn't want him to miss out on the adventures. Breaks in the school year for Barb and the kids meant the family packed into the car, with a small fold-up camper trailer in tow, and hit the road. The camper went with them everywhere, for thousands of miles across the United States. It had a stove that could be carried outside and hooked up to the side of the camper, something modern and unusual in those days. The first time the family went to Oregon, in 1968, people from all over the campground strolled the Hammonds' campsite to see the curious stove as Dick and Barb cooked hotdogs and burgers for the kids.

Dick usually took the family west of Illinois to vacation. He loved the mountains and the ocean, so any place was fine with him as long as one, or both, were included. They visited Maine, California, and Washington state—they drove into Canada sometimes as well. They visited with family on the West Coast, went camping in the Rocky Mountains, and drove to the Ruby Mountains. Dick felt it was especially important to take his family to visit Portland, Oregon. Dick had only lived in Portland briefly as a child, but the landscape had left a huge impression on him, and he wanted to make sure the children got to see the beauty it had to offer.

Dick was in the third grade when his family moved from Peoria to Portland. At the time, Dick's father was a tool designer. When he took a job with Hyster Manufacturing Company in Oregon, he packed the family up and headed west. It was only a year and a half later that Dick's father figured he was better off going back to Peoria to look for different work, and the family returned to Illinois. But Dick never forgot how much he loved being in Portland and how exquisite the scenery was to him. He loved the green lushness of the trees and the tranquility of the rivers. He loved the snow-topped mountain peaks and the deep blue-gray sea, which were so close in proximity to one another in that part of the world.

When Dick returned to Portland with his own family, he enjoyed showing them places that were familiar to him. He showed them the house that he lived in with his parents—it was much smaller than he remembered. He took them to Mount Hood. They hiked through the forests and visited the lakes. He showed the children the Columbia River and its waterfalls. He took his family to the Pacific Ocean, where from certain viewpoints, Dick could see just how near the coast and the mountains were to each other. He could stand in one spot and in front of him was the ocean and behind him were the mountains, and if he looked off to his side, he could see both at the same time, so close that it seemed as though they were touching. The mountains. The ocean. Together.

*

In 1970, a Catholic church did not exist in Bartonville, so every Sunday Dick and Barb traveled twenty minutes to the south end of Peoria to attend church. Getting the family ready for church was no small task. To simplify the process, Barb wrote down all the different schedules for Mass for every Catholic church on the south side of Peoria. Instead of making sure she had the children ready on time for a certain service, Barb would get the kids ready first and then determine which church they would be attending—early Mass at one church if the kids were dressed and fed early, or a later Mass at a different church if they

CHAPTER 2: DE

were running behind.

Dick and Barb wished a church was closer to their home so they wouldn't have to drive to Peoria each week, and they knew quite a few other families in Bartonville who felt the same. After some discussion, the families decided to form a group of interested community members to petition the bishop of the Peoria Diocese to establish a new church.

Dick and Barb dove headfirst into helping get petitions signed. After a few months of gaining support, the petitions were presented to the bishop. He agreed to back the new church and appointed a priest, Father Wellman, to lead the process. Dick and Barb were overjoyed by the bishop's decision to support the new church, but even more delighted about Father Wellman's appointment. They already knew Father Wellman from a church in Peoria, and they felt he was a great leader.

The bishop deemed the new church St. Anthony's Church, and Father Wellman formed a parish council. He began hosting Mass in the auditorium of a local hospital, which he continued to do for a few years until land was donated from the diocese for the construction of the new church's buildings. In 1972, the first building on the church's property, the liturgical center, was completed, and Dick and Barb, and the Catholic community of Bartonville, had a place to gather and worship, and call home.

Not long after the liturgical center was completed, Father Wellman and Dick were speaking with a visiting priest at the center, when Father Wellman introduced Dick as a "future permanent deacon." Dick was astounded. Later that day, he asked Father Wellman if he was serious, and he said he was. He thought Dick would make a good deacon, having seen him play an instrumental part in the establishment of St. Anthony's Church.

Dick had never considered a position as a deacon, and he wasn't even sure what exactly about him made Father Wellman think he would be good at it. But the seed had been planted in his mind, and Dick couldn't stop thinking about it. At home a few days later, he mentioned the conversation to Barb, and they talked about what Dick could offer to the Catholic Church. He knew he wanted to serve the community, and he and Barb started to feel like maybe it was his calling to become a deacon. Not long after, Dick applied for the diaconate program with the Roman Catholic Dioceses in Peoria. Nearly four years later, on December 12, 1976, he was ordained.

Dick enjoyed his role as a permanent deacon. He had no idea what he was capable of until he took on the task, and he found that he was able to do much more than he ever thought. He assisted Father Wellman with Mass, preached sermons, and taught classes at St. Anthony's Church. He loved participating in marriage ceremonies and family baptisms. He was pleased to be part of the clergy and was fond of participating in community celebrations. Some of those experiences, the marriages of their children and the baptisms of their grandchildren, became the most memorable of Dick's life.

*

When Dick and Barb stepped off the cruise ship in Port-au-Prince in 1974, they did not anticipate that what they would see would be so disturbing that they would return to the boat early. They knew a little about Haiti, but it had never resonated with Dick and Barb how poor the country actually was or what life was really like for Haitians.

To understand the plight of the Haitian people and the country, it is important to know the history of Haiti—so much

CHAPTER 2: DE

of the present situation is rooted in the past. Starting from its earliest days, Haiti's history reveals much about why today the country is plagued by poverty and political strife. Its history also gives insight into just how strong willed the Haitian people are, and how determined they are to survive.

In 1492, Christopher Columbus landed on an island in the Caribbean Sea, which he named "Hispaniola," current-day Haiti and the Dominican Republic. Inhabited by the Taíno civilization, the island was called Ayiti—"land of mountains"—by its natives. In the years after Columbus and his men claimed the land for Spain, a vast majority of the native people died as a result of assault, disease, and strain caused by slavery. By 1517, nearly ninety percent of the island's 250,000 indigenous inhabitants had perished.

In 1697, the Spanish ceded part of the island, which would later become the nation of Haiti, to the French, who named the new country Saint-Domingue. The independent nation, only six hundred miles from the United States and approximately equivalent in size to Massachusetts, would become an extremely valuable exporter in subsequent years. By the 1780s, the country was producing about one-third of the world's sugar and growing half of the world's coffee, supported by the vast amount of slave labor imported from Africa. As the demand for slave labor increased, Saint-Domingue became the chief port-of-call for slaves moving from Africa to the Americas. By 1789, the country was made up of roughly 55,000 free people and 450,000 slaves. The slave population was dying continuously from illness, brutality, and overwork. Deaths outnumbered births, but when addressing this rapid loss, plantation owners found it cheaper and easier to import new slaves instead of improving the lives of those already in the country. The slave population continued to increase, as the gap in numbers between the free people and the slaves grew even greater.

The free population and the slaves were not the only distinct castes within Saint-Domingue—the free population itself was divided by social class and status. Wealthy white planters, powerful officials, and poor white migrants made up the elite society. The others were referred to as "free people of color"— the non-whites who were not slaves, and sometimes even owned plantations, but who were considered to be of a lower class than their white counterparts. Free people of color where not allowed to hold certain jobs or administrative positions, and they were forced to abide by a different set of societal rules. Over time, the free people of color became increasingly disgruntled, demanding to be treated as equals. Finding their demands ignored, they revolted, with little success, their forces not large enough to outnumber the white population. But all of that changed when, in 1791, the slaves themselves banded together to fight the wealthy elite, resulting in the largest slave revolt in history.

Led by Toussaint Louverture, an educated former slave, the slave revolution successfully overpowered the white armies, aided in part by help from the free people of color who fought beside them. By 1801, Louverture was in complete control. The revolt was so successful that he not only took over Saint-Domingue, but all of Hispaniola, and he demanded the abolishment of slavery across the entire island. Back in France, Napoleon Bonaparte caught wind of Louverture's triumphs, and he ordered his brother-in-law, Captain Charles Leclerc, to attack Saint-Domingue and reestablish French rule, and slavery. Louverture was seized by Leclerc's troops and deported to France, where he died of pneumonia in a French prison in 1803.

Taking over in Louverture's absence was his lieutenant,

CHAPTER 2: DE

Jean-Jacques Dessalines, also a former slave, who continued to lead the fight against slavery, eventually defeating the powerful French army and leading the country to its independence. On January 1, 1804, Dessalines declared Saint-Domingue a sovereign nation and established "Haiti" as its official name, a modification of the spelling of the original name Ayiti. Haiti became the first independent nation in Latin America. Today, the Haitian Revolution remains the only successful slave revolt in history.

Haiti's newfound independence, however, was met with many challenges. Even after the abolition of slavery, a ruling elite remained. The free people of color were now considered part of the elite society, and the freed slaves remained peasants. The groups had differing opinions as to how the newly independent nation should compete within the global economy. The elites wanted the country to be a part of international trade, while the peasants wanted Haiti to produce its own goods and stay away from outside influence.

Even without the internal struggle, Haiti was already being disregarded in the global market. At the time, both Europe and the United States relied on slavery as a major economic stronghold, and without slave trade and slave labor in the country, Haiti was no longer of interest to governments there. The US government refused to officially recognize Haiti's existence, even though the United States had recently been selling more goods to Saint-Domingue than any other Latin American country. At the time of Haiti's independence, the US government placed an embargo on the nation and refused to officially acknowledge Haiti for more than fifty years—not until President Lincoln did so in 1862. Similarly, France refused to recognize Haiti as an independent nation until 1825, and then only under the condition that the Haitian government agree to offer compensation to French owners for the loss of plantations and the loss of slaves after the revolution. The French government demanded the Haitian government pay 150 million francs in reparations, equivalent to about twenty-one billion US dollars today. Haitian officials, desperate to be recognized so they could participate in the European market, agreed to pay back the debt to France, which, at the time, was one of the richest countries in the world. Haiti paid the debt to France for seventy-five years, until 1950.

*

For more than one hundred years after its independence, Haiti struggled as rival regimes and revolutionary armies forced leaders out of office continually. Political instability wreaked havoc on the country. As Haiti's political situation continued to decline into the twentieth century, assassinations became increasingly common. In 1915, President Woodrow Wilson staged an internal coup in an attempt to restore order. The US occupation would last until 1934. During that time, US banks took over Haiti's treasury, and the US Marines disbanded the Haitian army. Haitians met the occupation with resistance, and Haitian rebels fought the US army, leading to almost two decades of hostility within the country.

In the years following the US occupation, Haiti's leadership consisted mostly of a small number of families until, in 1957, François Duvalier was "selected" as president. Before getting involved in politics, Duvalier had been a physician. His patients affectionately called him Papa Doc, a moniker that stuck with him throughout his life. He served as the minister of health and labor in Haiti until 1956. While running for president, Duvalier was backed by the support of the Haitian military, and his only

CHAPTER 2: DE

political opponent had been forced into exile before the election, leaving him as the sole candidate in the running.

After elected, Duvalier instituted a new constitution and began his regime of terror. Wary of his control over the Haitian army, he created a militia called the Tonton Macoutes to enforce his power across the country. Named after the Haitian mythological bogeymen who kidnapped unruly children by sticking them into sacks in the night, the Macoutes grew in size to twice that of the army, operating as a sort of secret police. Under Duvalier's direction, they terrorized Haiti. All civic organizations in the country were disbanded, perceived as a potential threat to Duvalier's rule. The Macoutes attacked Haitians in broad daylight and abducted people they suspected were against Duvalier. It is estimated that during his fourteen-year presidency, nearly 30,000 Haitians were killed. Before his death in 1971, Duvalier, deeming himself "President for Life," changed Haitian law to allow his 19-year-old son, Jean-Claude "Baby Doc" Duvalier, to succeed him.

During the 1970s and 1980s, Haiti was in disarray. Baby Doc lived a lavish lifestyle as president while neglecting his role within the Haitian government. To make matters worse, the small tourist industry in Haiti was crippled when, in 1982, the US Centers for Disease Control released a report claiming the largest groups of AIDS victims was made up of homosexuals, heroin addicts, hemophiliacs, and Haitians. The label was unfair, and unwarranted, having been based solely on HIV/AIDS cases among Haitians who had migrated to the United States and not directly related to cases of Haitians actually living in Haiti. But the damage had already been done. After the report was published, charter flights discontinued service to Haiti. Cruise ships no longer docked in Port-a-Prince—the entire country became stigmatized by the virus.

The summer of 1984 saw food riots. Thousands of Haitians fled the country, escaping to the United States, Canada, the Dominican Republic, and France, as they desperately tried to find a better life outside of Haiti. In 1986, Baby Doc was overthrown by a popular uprising as Haitians became increasingly fed up with the state of their collapsed nation. He and his family where exiled to France, taking with them almost eighty million dollars in Haitian government funds. Even though 1986 marked the fall of the nearly thirty years of Duvalier dictatorship, it was not the end of Duvalierism—the country was left under the rule of the military junta, who continued to carry out atrocities against the Haitian people.

In the late 1980s and early 1990s, a priest by the name of Jean-Betrand Aristide became the voice for the opposition to the Duvalier regime. Aristide was born in Port-Salut, Haiti, in 1953. As a priest, he worked intensely for the poor. He gained popularity quickly, becoming increasingly known for his dedication to the dispossessed. In January 1991, Aristide was elected president by a landslide, winning sixty-seven percent of the vote in Haiti's first democratic election. But regardless of Aristide's popularity, the Haitian military and many of the Haitian elite opposed the new leader's attempt at reform within the government. Just seven months after his inauguration, in September 1991, Aristide's regime was toppled by a military coup, and the president was exiled, first to Venezuela, and then the United States.

In the years after Aristide's exile, the country was ruled by the Haitian army. The economy continued to worsen. In 1994, the Clinton administration intervened, and once again the United States occupied Haiti. In an attempt to restore constitutional rule,

CHAPTER 2: DE

Aristide was returned to Haiti on October 15, 1994, after more than three years of political exile, and reinstated as president. In 1995, at the end of his term, Aristide handed over the reins of power to René Préval, his former prime minister. Préval became the first Haitian president to serve his five-year term in its entirety until the next free presidential election. In 2000, Aristide was elected as president again, winning more than ninety percent of the vote.

By the early 2000s, Haiti was severely lacking in resources. The public sector could not provide even the most basic services to its citizens, including safe drinking water. Public health was poor, and the public education system was failing. In 2004, Aristide fled Haiti for a second time, after he was blamed for the assassination of a Haitian gang leader. Violent rebellions against him erupted as rebels invaded the capital. Fearful for his life, Aristide left the country, this time taking refuge in South Africa. In 2006, Haitian voters elected René Préval as president for his second term. That same year, Port-au-Prince was deemed the kidnapping capital of the world.

In April 2008, a worldwide spike in food and fuel prices lead to an increase in riots in Haiti. As a result of advanced deforestation in the country and widespread storms that struck throughout the year, landslides and floods devastated communities on the island. By 2009, half of school-aged children in Haiti were not attending school. The January 2010 earthquake ravaged Haiti—hundreds of thousands of people lost their lives, and over 1.5 million were left homeless. By October, a severe cholera outbreak affected over 700,000 Haitians and killed an estimated 9,000. In 2011, Michel Martelly, a former musician and a Haitian businessman, was elected president. Having come into office in the midst of great devastation, Martelly pledged to speed up reconstruction, but years after the earthquake, hundreds of thousands of Haitians remained in temporary shelters.

Today, Haiti remains vulnerable to natural disasters, as its people struggle with poverty, illness, and lack of governmental support. Still trying to rebuild after the earthquake, Haiti has seen some progress, but it has been slow, and tedious. Despite these circumstances, many Haitian people passionately love their country, its leaders, and its people. Even with all the difficulties of trying to survive among great obstacles, Haitians remain hopeful for the future.

*

After returning home from their cruise, Dick and Barb tried to forget about Haiti, even though they knew they had been greatly impacted by what they had seen. They couldn't imagine how anyone could begin to help in such a complicated place, so they put it out of their minds. It would be a few years before they came across the person who would make them think differently. Coincidentally, that person had been brought to Haiti for the first time the same way Dick and Barb had been—on a cruise ship. His name was Harry Hosey, and he would not only bring Dick back to Haiti for the second time, but he would pave the way for Dick and Barb's involvement with the Haitian people for the rest of their lives.

twa

This is my third mission trip to Haiti, and it still affects me. I think I know what I will see, but I never truly know what to expect. The poverty is unmatched by many other countries. Being a country with very little money means that the people will suffer with hardly anyone to help them. I'm told that some of the people that we see at the clinic have never seen any kind of doctor before. Ever.

Haiti is such a beautiful country that seems to be plagued with problems. But the Haitians are resilient people. Renel is one of the Haitian staff we work with at the clinic. No matter how bad things get, Renel always seems to be smiling. I have never seen him upset. He has been working to build a house, a small, bare structure he is so proud to own, something that most people would pay to give away in the United States. I'm happy to report that this year his house has had some improvements that mean the world to him—he now has a faucet that drips water from a pipe he hooked up about a half mile up the road. He has also started working on a bathroom, which will be a long and expensive process.

I would like to thank Dick and Barb Hammond for starting this clinic many years ago and growing it to what that it is today. People love to ask them about it, and they love telling the many stories they have under their belts. They love the Haitian people, as well as have respect for them. They are truly an inspiration to us all.

-Carlos, EMT
 September 2014

CHAPTER 3: TWA

Harry Hosey ended up in Nashville, Tennessee, by accident. Harry was born in the small farming town of Taber in Alberta, Canada, in 1912. As a teenager, he attended a seminary high school in Indiana. But before he graduated, he was asked to leave. The priest who ran the seminary didn't think Harry was cut out for the priesthood, even though he had always had a passion for the seminary's mission. Undaunted, Harry decided he would try another seminary school in Louisville, Kentucky, to finish his education. But while hitching a ride in the back of a truck to Louisville, Harry fell asleep, and the driver kept going right on through Kentucky, all the way to Nashville. When Harry woke up and realized where he was, he decided to stay in Tennessee, despite having only a few dollars in his pocket. Instead of returning to school, he found a job in sales, which ended up being a natural skill for him.

Harry met his first wife, Mary, in Nashville, and they had twelve children together. For several years, Harry worked as a life insurance salesman, until he needed a different profession to better support his large family. He started his own business manufacturing and selling laundry and dry cleaning supplies, which became successful rather quickly. A few years later, he purchased a house in Old Hickory, Tennessee, and moved his family out of the city and into the country onto a more rural piece of land. Around the same time, the US Army Corps of Engineers completed the Old Hickory Lake, which backed right up to the Hoseys' property. Harry developed part of the land into a beach. He named it Holiday Beach, and for ten years, during the summer months, the Hoseys opened their land to the public. They charged admission for swimming, sold concessions, and hosted luau parties, creating extra income for the family.

In 1951, tragedy struck the Hosey family when Mary died

during childbirth after having an allergic reaction to a medication given to her at the hospital. A year later, in 1952, Harry met his second wife, Alice. They soon married and she adopted all twelve of the children. Alice gave birth to two more children, making the Hosey brood a total of fourteen. The Hosey family would later joke that the priest from Harry's childhood had been right about Harry in the end—he was not cut out for the priesthood.

Throughout his life, Harry had a great love for his family and for the church. He had a huge desire to support mission work, a passion that would lead him to develop projects in Haiti for decades. And because he was such a persistent businessman, Harry would prove himself adept at convincing others to get involved in the work he had become so passionate about. He was lighthearted and had a good sense of humor. But, without a doubt, as Dick would come to find out, Harry had a little devil in him too.

In 1956, just as Dick and Barb would do almost two decades later, Harry and Alice went on a Caribbean cruise that docked in Port-au-Prince. When they arrived, they avoided the usual tourist destinations and ventured off by themselves to visit the capital's slums. They found the conditions in Port-au-Prince worse than Harry had expected. Because of what they had seen, he and Alice were determined to one day come back to help.

It didn't take Harry long to return. He was home for less than a year before making his way back to Haiti in 1957 in search of mission work to pursue full time. In the years that followed, both he and Alice returned to Haiti as they became involved in various projects, but it was Harry who visited most often by far. He was undeniably drawn to Haiti, and he visited every chance he could. He loved everything about the country. He loved the atmosphere and the rich culture, he loved the spirit of the churches, and he

CHAPTER 3: TWA

loved the people. He felt at home in Haiti more than anywhere else, and because of that, he visited more than sixty times in his life.

One of the first projects Harry and Alice undertook was selling linens for a Belgian nun, Sister Pia. Sister Pia belonged to a church in Port-au-Prince that employed women to make linens, which they then sold as a source of income. Harry and Alice would travel to Haiti to collect the linens and then sell them in Tennessee to help the women and Sister Pia's church. They eventually became involved with other churches in Haiti and started taking on bigger projects—they helped build schools, houses, and dispensaries. They also distributed funds collected from their church at home to give to priests in Haiti for pastoral needs.

In the mid-1970s, after traveling to Haiti for nearly twenty years, Harry realized he and Alice could no longer support numerous projects alone. Harry encouraged his church in Nashville to get involved with some of their efforts. During a presentation to the congregation about their work in Haiti, Harry's stories got the attention of a parishioner named Theresa Patterson. Theresa became so interested in his cause that she asked if she could join Harry the next time he visited Haiti. Later that year, she accompanied Harry to Beauchamp, in Haiti's Nord-Ouest department, where they visited churches and talked to priests to get a better idea of the specific needs of the Haitian people. While on their trip, Harry and Theresa discussed the possibility of getting other churches back in the United States, outside of their own, involved in missionary efforts in Haiti. They decided that after returning Theresa would petition the Diocese of Nashville for support, and Harry would reach out to parishes outside of the state.

Out of their newfound partnership, Harry and Theresa created the Parish Twinning Program of the Americas (PTPA), linking Catholic parishes in the United States with parishes in Haiti. Through the program, US parishes provided monetary support for parishes in Haiti for religious, educational, and medical needs—a kind of "adoption" program. Harry and Theresa worked hard to expand their programs, and eventually it led to partnerships with parishes all over the Caribbean and Latin America. Almost forty years after Harry and Theresa visited Haiti together for the first time, the PTPA now has more than 350 parish linkages in existence.

*

It was 1978 when Barb first became familiar with the PTPA. One evening while she was thumbing through a magazine, she came across an article on Harry Hosey and his work. She was immediately intrigued. She related to the article's description of how Harry felt after visiting Haiti for the first time—his experience seeing the poverty in Port-au-Prince and the feeling of wanting to do something. Dick and Barb had had the same feeling, but they had never known what to do about it—they never felt that there was anything they could do, so they went back to living their lives as usual. Suddenly, she thought they might be able to help.

The next day, Barb called the PTPA office to find out how she could get St. Anthony's Church involved. Harry answered the phone. He was so enthusiastic about Barb's interest in the PTPA, he suggested meeting her and Dick. He would gladly make the drive to Bartonville, along with Alice, to talk with them in person. Barb was surprised Harry wanted to make such a long trip—they were complete strangers. But she was eager to ask

CHAPTER 3: TWA

more questions about the PTPA programs, and since Harry was so animated on the phone, she agreed to the visit.

A few weeks later, Harry and Alice made the eight-hour drive from Nashville to Bartonville. Dick and Barb were nervous about what to anticipate from the meeting but also hopeful. This could be a real way for them to get involved in helping in Haiti. When Harry and Alice arrived to the house, they all greeted each other warmly. Harry expressed his sincerest gratitude for Dick and Barb's interest. Dick and Barb loved Harry's energy immediately and could tell he was a kind and trustworthy person, which put them at ease. As they made their way to the living room to sit down, Harry started explaining how the PTPA worked.

With a parish adoption, no set amount of money was required to be sent, and the donated funds would go straight to the adopted parish. Harry assured Dick and Barb the funds were being used appropriately, because he visited the parishes himself—he traveled extensively between the United States and Haiti making sure that the parish adoption relationships were fully developed. He had gotten to know the priests in all the parishes well, ensuring they understood how the program worked and what the funds were to be used for. Alice sat next to Harry, nodding in approval, as Dick and Barb listened. With each moment, their apprehension eased, and their excitement grew. Harry's enthusiasm was contagious.

Even before Harry finished talking, Dick and Barb knew they wanted to get St. Anthony's Church involved, and they wanted to support a parish in Haiti where the need was the greatest. Harry knew of the exact parish to suggest. St. Dominic's Parish was located in Marigot, in the Sud-Est department, about ninety kilometers south of Port-au-Prince, near a town called Jacmel. St. Dominic's parish had eight chapels and only one priest. Needless to say, this priest was handling a great deal on his own, and Harry knew he could use the financial support.

That priest's name was Father Michel LaBourne. A French priest who attended seminary and priest training in France, Father LaBourne had moved to Haiti after finishing his training. When Harry met him, he had been living in Haiti for about fifteen years. Father LaBourne resided in the rectory at St. Dominic's Church, the main church in Marigot. When it came to his involvement with the people in the parish, Father LaBourne was particularly interested in supporting the education of the Haitian children. With financial assistance, Father LaBourne had explained to Harry, he could establish schools within the churches and afford to purchase supplies and pay teacher salaries.

After Harry and Alice left their house later that evening, Dick and Barb didn't waste any time making a plan to stir up support within St. Anthony's Church. Within a few days, they talked to the parish council about the PTPA, and the council agreed to support the parish adoption. Barb also spoke with the church congregation, explaining how their donations would provide for educational programs in Haiti. She held bake sales, and yard sales, and more yard sales, and then more bake sales to raise money. Within the church, a special envelope was designated so church members could donate as they wished.

Nine months after Dick and Barb meet with Harry and Alice, St. Anthony's Church was finally ready to start sending funds to St. Dominic's Church in Marigot. St. Anthony's Church was the first church to adopt a parish on the southern coast of Haiti, and the first in the state of Illinois to adopt through the PTPA.

*

More than a year later, the St. Anthony's parish adoption was

CHAPTER 3: TWA

running smoothly, and Dick and Barb were rarely in contact with Harry. They didn't need to be in touch with him—he was busy expanding the PTPA programs, and Dick and Barb had gone back to their equally busy lives with family and work. So when the phone rang one evening, Barb was surprised to hear Harry's voice on the other end. Dick could hear her talking from the next room.

"Well, we can't do that. No, we just can't do that, Harry," Dick listened to Barb saying over and over.

They continued back and forth for a while. After some time, Dick grew tired of listening outside of the conversation, and took the phone from Barb.

"Harry?" Dick said, slightly irritated.

"Dick!" Harry exclaimed, ignoring Dick's tone. "I want you to go to Haiti."

"What for?" Dick asked, taken aback by Harry's seemingly out-of-the-blue proposal.

"Well, since St. Anthony's Church has been supporting St. Dominic's Parish for some time now, I think you should go to Haiti and meet Father LaBourne."

Dick wasted no time in giving his answer. "No!" he told Harry, firmly.

Dick told Harry there was no way he was going to Haiti. He was busy with work and Barb was teaching, and the kids were in school. He couldn't be away from home. International travel was simply out of the question. But Harry was unwavering. He again pressed Dick to consider making the trip. Dick refused his request once more, said goodnight, and hung up the phone.

But Dick had a feeling Harry did not take his answer seriously. What he didn't realize at the time was that Harry was an unrelenting salesman, and he would not stop until he sold

Dick on the idea of going to Haiti. Over the next few weeks, Harry, along with Alice, called Dick and Barb's house every few days, badgering Dick about meeting Father LaBourne in person. Eventually, Dick grew tired of arguing with Harry and started to listen to his reasoning. Harry explained that he wanted Dick to see how the funds St. Anthony's Church was sending were being used and how it was truly helping with the children's educational needs. It was important to Harry that Dick and Barb retained their interest in supporting St. Dominic's Parish. And besides, Father LaBourne could use the help of a deacon like Dick with his parish duties. He was handling more weddings and baptisms and masses than one priest should on his own.

What Harry didn't say to Dick was that his plea was a part of a larger plan. Harry had a feeling that Dick was capable of doing more than just supporting a parish from home. If he could convince Dick to go to Haiti, he thought Dick would see something special in the people of the country and the spirituality of the Haitians, just as Harry had years before. And then, hopefully, Dick would realize he wanted to get more involved in working in Haiti—maybe even do something big.

After weeks of pestering, Dick finally gave up and agreed to travel to Marigot for a four-day weekend, mostly just to get Harry and Alice to leave him alone. Harry was ecstatic. He told Dick to go ahead and make arrangements to leave in the next few weeks. He and Alice would already be in Haiti by the time Dick arrived, and they would pick him up at the François Duvalier International Airport (later to become the Toussaint Louverture International Airport) in Port-au-Prince. They would all stay the night in the city and the next day drive the few hours south to Marigot.

As Dick prepared to return to Haiti, something he thought he

CHAPTER 3: TWA

would never do, he became increasingly nervous thinking about what might happen to him. He knew Haiti could be a dangerous place to visit—he was familiar with the political state of the country under Baby Doc's rule, and he figured he could be a target just as much as anyone else.

The night before he left, he carefully packed boxes of donated items that Barb had collected from the St. Anthony's Church congregation to take with him. As he arranged the clothes, shoes, and medications like pain relievers and vitamins that he would soon be distributing to Haitians in Marigot, he thought about whom he might meet in Haiti, and what he might see. He became more anxious as he packed his personal belongings, not knowing exactly what to bring for himself. He realized he didn't know what he would be doing while he was there. He didn't know what the agenda was at all. He was blindly following Harry's lead. Dick became increasingly concerned about relying completely on someone else to make plans for him, and, even though he trusted Harry, he wasn't sure what he was getting himself into.

Before leaving, Dick spoke to Harry one last time on the phone, just to make sure everything was in order before he departed. Harry told him not to worry about traveling to Haiti alone—everything would be fine.

Worried was exactly what he should have been.

*

It was 1980. Dick was heading to Haiti for the second time in his life. While on the flight from Miami to Port-au-Prince, Dick sat behind two men traveling with a missionary group. He could clearly hear their conversation, which was one he would never forget. The two men were busy discussing how much peanut brittle they had brought with them. Dick gathered that they had prepared the peanut brittle to give to the Haitians while the missionaries built some sort of structure. Their plan was to keep the Haitians, adults and children alike, occupied with sweet treats while the Americans worked.

Dick couldn't believe what he was hearing. He didn't understand why they had picked peanut brittle of all things—something with limited nutritional value that would rot their teeth. But more importantly, he was bothered that the two men seemed to have no intention of involving any Haitians with the construction project. Surely, Dick thought to himself, the Haitians would know more than the Americans about building in their own country—which materials to use, what construction equipment was available, and where to get supplies. Dick was baffled, bristling at their arrogance.

When the plane arrived, Dick headed to baggage claim to gather his bags and boxes before he went through customs. Harry had warned him before he left that if he packed the boxes so that the usable goods were on top, Haitian customs workers might confiscate those items. Customs in the Port-au-Prince airport checked everything coming in and sometimes removed things with no explanation. It made it difficult to fly anything useful into Haiti, especially medications. At Harry's suggestion, Dick had put a false bottom in the boxes. After searching and finding nothing other than clothes, the customs agents let him go, motioning him toward the airport exit. Dick, pleased that Harry's idea had worked, picked up his belongings, and headed out of the airport.

As soon as Dick walked through the exit doors into the stagnant heat of the early evening, he was engulfed in disarray. His memory of the crowds in Port-au-Prince came back to him as his eyes darted around, searching for Harry and Alice among

CHAPTER 3: TWA

the faces. The airport was swamped with cars and motorbikes. Family members waited for the arrival of other passengers, pressed tightly against a small barrier outside the main doors. Immediately, a group of Haitian tap tap drivers surrounded Dick from all sides, loudly competing for his attention. Ready to make a quick buck from a tourist, the men offered to carry his luggage or give him a ride. Dick didn't see Harry or Alice anywhere as he scanned the parking lot—he had expected them to be waiting right out front.

Dick found a spot on the sidewalk a small distance away from the crowd to set his things down as he waited. The tap tap drivers continued to follow him closely, all frantically vying to win him over. The men even tried to pick up Dick's boxes while grabbing his arm, trying to lead him toward their vehicles. He kept telling them that someone was coming to pick him up, that he didn't need a ride, that he was fine. He repeated himself to no avail. The tap tap drivers persisted.

"Let me take you to a hotel," one Haitian man said in halting English.

"That makes no sense. Harry won't know where I am," Dick responded, confused and overwhelmed.

"Oh, he will find you, don't worry, we know where to take you, he will find you," insisted another driver. Dick thought, *I'm dumb, but I'm not that dumb.* He knew these men didn't know who Harry was, nor did they have any idea where he was staying that night—Dick didn't even know where he was staying that night. He didn't have a phone number to try to get in touch with Harry, nor a clue where a phone might be anyway. As time went by, he grew increasingly concerned about why Harry was so late. He didn't know what he would do if he didn't show up. He was completely alone and didn't know where to go.

A few hours had gone by. It was getting later and later in the evening. The sun had set, and the day was turning into night. Lights began to turn off—first inside the terminal, and then outside along the one road traveling in and out of the airport. Traffic was thinning out and eventually disappeared as the last plane took off for the day. The crowd of passengers and family members went home, and the tap tap drivers, giving up on Dick, scattered off to try to drum up business elsewhere. Dick was the only one left. His worry was turning into panic.

All of a sudden, he saw headlights beaming in his direction. It was a small car, puttering down the road into the airport, at a dull, slow speed. The vehicle drove up to the sidewalk where he was standing, and the driver's-side window rolled down. Inside sat Harry and Alice.

"Hi Dick!" said Harry, without a hint of an apology.

Dick was fuming, even though he was relieved to see Harry.

"Damn it, Harry!" Dick said, his fists clenched by his side. He couldn't believe Harry had enticed him to leave home, promising him everything was ready for him, and then hadn't even picked him up from the airport on time. Harry turned his head away from Dick and looked over at Alice in the passenger seat.

"See, I told you, Harry," Alice said, very matter of fact. "I said he was going to be mad at you, and I was right."

"What the heck happened?" Dick pleaded, desperately wanting an explanation for their tardiness.

"Oh, I just forgot," Harry said, with an air of casualness. He was either unaware of, or simply choosing to ignore, Dick's anger. "Get in, Dick!"

Dick threw his things into the backseat and got into the car. He slumped in his seat, visibly upset about Harry's forgetfulness, and he insisted he be taken to the guesthouse right away. He was

CHAPTER 3: TWA

exhausted and ready to be by himself for the night so he could get some rest.

Harry pulled away from the curb, leaving the now-vacant airport behind. Unbeknownst to Dick, however, they were not headed to the guesthouse. Harry had a different plan in mind for when Dick arrived in Haiti. He started driving towards an area of Port-au-Prince called Cité Soleil (Sun City), located just west of the airport. The largest slum in the city, Cité Soleil's residents are among the most impoverished in the area. They are the poorest of the poor, and the conditions they live in are harsh—they have no functioning sewer system and virtually no electricity. Many of the homes are made of scavenged material—scrap wood and old tarps and sheets of rusty metal. The dwellings are built so closely together that one would have to turn sideways to walk between the small shacks. The slum is densely populated, with an estimated 200,000 to 400,000 residents, many of whom are unemployed. Violence is rampant as gangs roam the streets.

Not long after leaving the airport, Harry pulled off the main road, entering Cité Soleil. He drove down a muddy, unpaved street and then stopped under a streetlight, which was nothing more than a bulb hanging off a wire attached to a thin tree. It shone only the slightest amount of light onto the car—otherwise, the street was completely dark. He put the car in park, cut off the engine, and turned around to face Dick.

"Dick, I want to tell you about this place," he began.

"Harry, I just want to go to bed," Dick grumbled, still irritable after being left at the airport to fend for himself.

"This won't take long," Harry said calmly, turning to look out of the windshield and into the night.

Harry spoke slowly as they sat in the car, in the dark of the street, in one of the biggest slums in the Northern Hemisphere.

Haitians walked by, looking through the windows, curious as to what the *blancs*, the white people, were doing there so late in the evening. Dick could see that they were visibly thin, and the children wore dirty clothes. Many of them went without shoes. Harry didn't pay much attention to the Haitians passing by the car as he described the scene to Dick. He pointed out the rundown shacks, no bigger than an American bathroom, and the filthy streets where the children played during the day. He talked about how the Haitians lived, without adequate food, water, or sanitation. He described how they feared for their safety and how they had little hope for a better future, and little opportunity to get out of poverty. He told a story about a priest that fed people rice and beans on a daily basis, so that a few hundred of the tens of thousands of Haitians living in Cité Soleil would receive at least one meal a day. Harry's speech lasted nearly forty-five minutes. When he was satisfied that he had shown Dick destitution like he had never seen before, he started the car and drove out of the slum.

At first, while Harry was talking, all Dick could think about was how tired he was, and how he wanted to get out of there as soon as he could. It was scary and intimidating to be brought to the slums, especially after having been left at the airport. Dick didn't realize then that the stop in Cité Soleil had been a part of Harry's plan all along. The first thing he felt Dick needed to understand was what life was like in Haiti for so many Haitian people, and, to do so, Harry felt Dick needed to see it for himself.

Harry continued to drive through Port-au-Prince, up narrow roads, winding through the hills. Electricity was spotty at best, making the city seem even more desolate than it already felt in the quiet night. As Harry drove slowly and carefully, Dick

CHAPTER 3: TWA

saw children out in the streets, standing under the few working streetlights. He noticed a couple of the children were holding books, and he assumed they were reading their homework assignments for the day. Dick was impressed and touched. He couldn't imagine how they could learn like that—leaning against a pole in almost complete darkness. He didn't understand how they could ever be good students if that was how they studied every evening. The image of seeing the children trying so hard to learn would stick in his mind for a long time to come.

When they arrived at the guesthouse, the whole place was dark. Harry and Alice were staying somewhere else, but Harry assured Dick that it would be fine—they themselves had stayed at this particular house before, and he knew it was safe. Dick took only what he needed for the night, and the rest of the supplies stayed in the car. Harry walked him to his room.

"I will see you in the morning. Be out on the street at the crack of dawn," he said.

"Are you sure, Harry? I don't want another bad experience like tonight. I am not built to put up with this type of stuff," Dick replied.

"Don't worry, Dick. I won't forget you," Harry said, smiling, as he turned to head back to the car.

Inside the room, Dick shut the door and sat down on the bed. He didn't know whether or not to believe Harry. Again finding himself alone and unsure, he wondered what he was doing so far from home. Not much had given him the confidence he made the right decision to return to Haiti. Dick cleaned up and got into bed, but he couldn't sleep. He was shaken by the circumstances of the day and was feeling vulnerable. Just outside of his room it was dangerous, and the threats were real. The Tonton Macoutes, the bogeymen, with sunglasses and machetes, were out there.

After some time, Dick fell asleep, anxiously anticipating what was in store for him in the next few days.

*

In the morning, Dick was out on the road by dawn as Harry had instructed. As he stood on the street waiting to be picked up, he had a chance to see Haiti in the light of the morning. People were starting their days just as soon as the sun was up. Women with baskets on their heads walked by on their way to the market. Children in uniforms with book bags slung over their shoulders ran past as they hurried to get to school. Some men hauled sugarcane in carts as others guided livestock down the road. Motorbikes and colorfully painted tap tap buses overflowing with passengers filled the road.

Not a soul went by that didn't greet Dick. Everyone smiled, nodded, and said a polite, *Bonjou*, "Good morning," to him. Dick waved and smiled back. Everything was peaceful. Dick had been so scared ever since he arrived. He had been uncomfortable with how unfamiliar it all was to him. But on this simple, routine morning in Haiti, Dick was seeing something completely different than he had before. His surroundings were pleasant. He was getting a sense that Haitians were happy people despite the difficulties he knew they faced. Despite the fact that they lived in fear of their own government. Despite the fact that they struggled daily in ways that were hard for him to imagine, the Haitians he saw were warm and friendly. Dick felt at ease.

When Harry and Alice arrived fifteen minutes later, Harry announced that before driving to Marigot, they were going to Mass at a Catholic church close by, followed by breakfast with a group of priests from Port-au-Prince. He explained that the priests were associated with a few of the parishes adopted by the

CHAPTER 3: TWA

PTPA, and he wanted Dick to meet them. Dick tried to protest, not wanting to get off track from meeting Father LaBourne in Marigot, but Harry didn't seem to hear him. Whether Harry was listening or not, Dick was starting to notice that this was part of Harry's personality, and he was going to have to learn to accept that things were going to go according to Harry's plans.

After Mass, a breakfast of fruit and toast was served at the church rectory. Dick sat down at the table with Harry and Alice and the priests. After a few moments listening to the priests' conversation, Dick realized they were all speaking Haitian Creole, the official language of the country. It occurred to him that it was going to be difficult to understand what was being discussed for the duration of the meal, and maybe even for the rest of his trip. He instantly felt isolated and intimidated. He became self-conscious, thinking the priests were possibly talking about him, maybe wondering who he was and why he was eating with them. Harry and Alice did not speak Creole either, but they didn't seem to mind that they didn't understand the conversation. Dick would later joke that he thought Harry was only there to get a free breakfast.

After they finished eating, Dick was pleased that it was finally time to go meet Father LaBourne. But once again, Harry had a change of plans. They would not be meeting Father LaBourne in Marigot as Dick had thought—they would be meeting him at a church in Jacmel, fourteen miles from Marigot. Dick didn't even bother protesting. At this point, he was along for the ride and ready for whatever was going to come his way. And even though Dick wouldn't admit it until years later, he was having a nice time with Harry and Alice. All Harry wanted to do was show him as much as possible in the brief time he was in Haiti and make sure that it left a lasting impression on Dick—and it did.

Jacmel is the largest town in Haiti's Sud-Est department. A vibrant place, with brightly colored buildings and a lively art and cultural scene, it is considered one of the safest tourist destinations in the country. The many galleries and artesian shops in Jacmel sell paintings and wood carved animal figures. Tourists visiting will also see the popular local flair of papier-mâché masks for Carnival lining the walls of the shops. Jacmel is widely known in Haiti for Carnival, a celebration leading up to Mardi Gras each year, and the event attracts thousands of Haitians and foreigners to participate in parades with festive music and dancing.

As Harry drove out of Port-au-Prince, heading south towards Jacmel, the road curved along the meandering mountainsides of Haiti's terrain. Dick thought the drive was beautiful. As he looked out into the countryside, the hills rolled and bowed as the car careened around each bend, up and down, up and down. He stared out the window and saw cows, goats, pigs, and chickens walking along the side of the road, right next to Haitians heading to the market or to work in the fields. Outside of the city, Haiti was calm, and quiet. No longer feeling anxious, Dick was at peace with the unknown awaiting.

kat

Today, I am here in Haiti attempting to bring knowledge and medical care to individuals who have limited or no access to resources, which are basic essentials in my life at home, such as water, food, and shelter.

As a pediatrician and human, I come to Haiti because it settles my mind and quiets my heart to hear the voices of those who are not heard. It reminds me of how important it is to listen and acknowledge the needs of others whether their request can be resolved or not.

Acknowledging what can be done or not done for someone is a reality throughout the entire world. It is a reality that I deal with as I see a child with developmental regression that I cannot do anything for, except educate the mother about exercises and tasks she can perform on a daily basis to encourage that child to reach his or her full potential.

The Haitians embrace every little thing that is provided to them as an opportunity that has opened up to them that they didn't have before. It may be as simple as providing them with a multivitamin, a bar of soap, hypertension medication, or diabetes education.

Embrace opportunities to help those in need.

-Chris, DO (Doctor of Osteopathy)
November 2011

CHAPTER 4: KAT

To this day, Dick doesn't know if Harry was trying to mislead him, or just wasn't paying attention to his question, but when Dick asked if Father LaBourne spoke English, Harry said yes. That wasn't exactly true—in fact, it wasn't true at all. Father LaBourne didn't speak any English.

Father LaBourne was a Frenchman. He was a small, soft-spoken man, who never raised his voice in conversation. When Dick met him, he was in his early forties, almost the same age as Dick. He spoke French and Creole, the latter of which he learned while attending seminary. He was from an order of priests whose sole purpose was to work in Haiti, and it would be the only place he ever served. Father LaBourne had seven adopted Haitian children he, along with his housekeeper, a Haitian woman named Lorriane, cared for. They all lived in the rectory of St. Dominic's Church.

In the early afternoon, a few hours after they had left Port-au-Prince, Harry, Alice, and Dick reached the church in Jacmel. They got out of the car and mingled about while they waited for Father LaBourne, who pulled up to the church in his car a short while later. He got out to greet them, saying *Bonswa*, "Good Afternoon," as he reached out his hand toward Harry. Harry understood what Father LaBourne had said and shook his hand. Harry then turned to introduce Dick. Confused, Dick went along with the introduction, shaking Father LaBourne's hand as he politely smiled. Following a few short exchanges of words in English and Creole, and nods and smiles, Harry said goodbye to Father LaBourne. Eager to continue with other PTPA business, he and Alice headed back to their car.

Dick, confused, followed, catching up with Harry. "Wait a minute, Harry. I am going to be with this guy, by myself, and he doesn't speak English?" he asked. Dick did not understand how he was going to be of any help to Father LaBourne if they could not understand one another.

"Don't worry, Dick. You're going to be fine," Harry said, ignoring Dick's concern, as he opened the car door and pulled out Dick's bags and boxes of donations, setting them down on the ground.

Before Harry left, he explained to Dick what he had gathered from Father LaBourne about their schedule for the weekend. Once again, the trip to Marigot to see St. Dominic's Church would be postponed. Instead, they were to go to Marbial, about six or seven miles northeast of Jacmel, for Feast Day. During Feast Day, the priests from all the parishes in the area gathered at a certain church to celebrate Mass together, and it was important for Father LaBourne to be present. After Feast Day was over, Father LaBourne and Dick would then be on their way to Marigot.

Dick couldn't believe it—at this point, he still would not be going to Marigot for a few more *days*. His scheduled four days in Haiti was not going to be enough. Before Harry left, Dick asked him to call Barb on his behalf to let her know he would be staying longer than he originally anticipated. Dick knew St. Dominic's Parish was large, and if he was going to see any of it, he was going to need to extend his trip.

Dick loaded his things into Father LaBourne's car, and they headed out of Jacmel toward Marbial. As they drove, the road led them through the Grande Rivière de Jacmel, which, at the time, was not much of a river at all. It was the dry season, and the river was nothing more than a rocky stream, shallow enough to be passable by car. Father LaBourne stopped the vehicle and looked out through the passenger-side window past Dick, pointing to a cornfield in the distance.

CHAPTER 4: KAT

"Mayi," said Father LaBourne.

Dick looked to where he was pointing and turned back to look at him.

"Corn," said Dick. They both laughed, and Father LaBourne continued driving.

Dick and Father LaBourne had communicated despite their language barrier. It was their first small bit of communication, which would develop for many years and become part of a special way they corresponded with one another. Barb would later describe their relationship as quite unbelievable—they never spoke the same language but they were always in sync. Dick and Father LaBourne used hand gestures and facial expressions to get their point across, and they became so good at communicating, even a translator would be behind on their conversations.

*

The drive from Jacmel to Marbial took about an hour. Dick and Father LaBourne arrived at a small church where the Feast Day celebration was being held and went inside the parish hall to meet the other priests, all of whom were French, with the exception of one Haitian priest, a pastor of a church in Jacmel.

After being introduced, Dick rested at the rectory of the church while Father LaBourne continued his conversations with the other priests, talking about the issues in their own parishes. When dinner was served a few hours later, Dick joined the priests in the church rectory. He was seated next to the Haitian priest he had met earlier. His name was Father Redori, and he spoke Creole and English.

"Are you American? Do you speak Creole?" Father Redori asked Dick.

Dick told him he only spoke English.

Father Redori smiled widely. "I speak English too!"

"You sure do!" Dick said, overjoyed. "I haven't been able to speak to any of the priests since I got here. Nobody understands what I am saying."

Father Redori assured Dick he would translate for him the best he could. Dick relaxed immediately. Over dinner, Father Redori translated the other priests' conversations for Dick, as well as explained how the priests in the local parishes handled visiting so many churches. Each week, they rotated which churches they visited in their own parishes, visiting one church a week, until they had visited every church in the parish, and then they would start over. Since the priests were not scheduled to be back at any one church for many weeks at a time, multiple marriages and baptisms were often scheduled on the same day. On top of all the ceremonies, they were also responsible for holding Mass and hearing confessions. They were indeed busy, just as Harry had said.

After dinner, the priests all retired for the evening, and Dick went to his room to get some rest. It had been a long day, and he was exhausted, but also pleased with how things were turning out, especially since Father Redori had been able to clarify so much for him. The next morning, Dick got up early to prepare for Mass. As soon as he was dressed, he met Father LaBourne outside of the church. Father LaBourne positioned Dick as cross bearer in the procession, making him one of the first to enter the church. When he walked through the doors of the church, he could see that it was packed inside. Hundreds of Haitians filled the benches and lined the walls. They spilled out of the doors and leaned in through the windows. It was amazing. As Dick walked by, every Haitian he passed reached out to touch him gently and affectionately. He had never experienced anything like

CHAPTER 4: KAT

it before.

When it came time for Communion, Dick stationed himself for distribution. But the priests soon realized they had a problem—they had not consecrated enough altar breads for the enormous crowd. They gathered to discuss how they should proceed. The priests did not want to disappoint anyone, so they decided to run through the consecration again so that everyone could receive Communion.

After the second consecration, Dick was directed to stand by a side door so he could reach the Haitians outside the church. A Haitian nun brought people to him one by one as he distributed altar breads. The crowd was immense. It just seemed to go on forever. Dick was stunned to see the number of people who wanted to participate. And every Haitian he saw reached out to grab onto him in a loving and caring way. They touched him gently on his arm, or held onto his hand to show how grateful they were for him to visit Haiti and come to their church. Dick had never felt so loved, least of all by strangers. He knew he was getting to be a part of something special. He would never forget his first Mass in Haiti. For him, it was one of the most touching experiences of his life. The Haitian people were so in tune with being a part of Communion, and it moved him beyond words.

When Mass was over, Dick, Father LaBourne, and Father Redori spoke to a few church members who mingled about after the service. Father Redori introduced Dick to a Haitian man who had asked to meet him. The gentleman was well dressed and proud to tell Dick about his job. He was a senator and the church was part of his jurisdiction. He talked about his son, who was in the United States working as a doctor. The senator boasted about how successful his son was working outside of Haiti. Dick asked the senator why his son did not work in the country where he was born.

The senator replied, "There is no money in helping his people."

Dick was discouraged by the senator's answer. Finding out that Haitians who were fortunate enough to get an education and become doctors did not even want to work in Haiti and help their own people was deeply disturbing for Dick. If Haitian doctors didn't want to work in Haiti, what doctors did?

*

The next day, with the Feast Day celebration behind them, it was time for Dick and Father LaBourne to go to Marigot. At last, Dick was going to see St. Dominic's Church. Before they left, Father Redori said he would like to go with them to translate for Dick. Dick was elated. Not only were they finally going to St. Dominic's, but now he would be able to understand so much more with Father Redori along. As the men left in Father LaBourne's car, Dick's spirits were high.

When they arrived a few hours later, Father LaBourne pulled through the iron gates of St. Dominic's Church, and parked outside of the church rectory. He took Dick inside where he met Lorriane, whose warm smile and cheerful demeanor struck him immediately. Not only did Lorriane take care of the rectory and the church, she also cooked, did the laundry, and made sure Father LaBourne's children were fed and went to school. She was also in charge of Father LaBourne's schedule, making his appointments so he knew which church he was visiting on which particular day or week. She welcomed Dick into their home, delighted to have a guest, as well as someone to help Father LaBourne with his duties.

Father LaBourne then showed Dick to his guest room. It

CHAPTER 4: KAT

was small, with only a bed and one open window, but it was comfortable, and more than enough room for him alone. After he unpacked, Dick went back outside, eager to walk around the property of St. Dominic's Church, which he had waited so long to see. He walked passed the parish hall. It was sizable, but basic—made from concrete, with six doors and windows on all sides. He noticed the church was directly in front of the rectory. An old stone and block building with a metal roof, the church was marked on the front with three large metal doors. On the sides of the building, the windows were nothing more than openings in the walls, allowing for sunlight and air to flow freely. Dick thought it was a nice church. It was much larger than the church in Marbial—soon he would find out that St. Dominic's Church was one of the nicer, and bigger, churches in the whole parish. Many of the smaller, poorer communities had churches that were nothing more than thatched-roof huts with no walls and dirt floors, which offered standing room only, barely big enough to cover more than a few dozen people. St. Dominic's had a concrete floor and could easily hold three hundred or more.

Dick walked up the few stairs that led into the church. Inside were rows of wooden pews and folding chairs. The walls of the church were painted a gentle light blue. A white stone altar stood at the front of the church, with a lace cloth gently laid across the length of it. A simple wooden cross hung on the wall behind the altar. All in all, it took only a couple of minutes to see the few buildings that made up St. Dominic's Church. It was as plain as Dick had expected it to be, yet it was lovely, and Dick walked out feeling content to have seen it for himself after such a long trip to get there.

It had already begun to get dark outside by the time Dick

headed back to the rectory for the night. As he approached the building, he walked under a wide oak tree. Just as he did, the tree began to shake. He paused, and the shaking stopped. Then he moved again, and the tree shook again, this time more aggressively. Dick was scared. He looked up, terrified, only to see turkeys roosting on the branches above his head. He was relieved to see only birds, but after getting startled like that, he knew that in certain ways he still felt uneasy, even though he was much more relaxed than when he first arrived in Haiti.

The next morning, Dick woke at sunrise, and before he even had a chance to raise his head from the pillow, a chicken flew in the small open window next to his bed. It walked around for a moment, then jumped back up and flew away. Less on edge in the daylight, Dick thought it was funny to have a chicken fly in his room, making the scare he got from the turkeys the night before seem that much more ridiculous.

After breakfast in the rectory, Father LaBourne drove Dick and Father Redori around Marigot to show them the town. Marigot is a small fishing community, with probably fewer than a thousand residents. Dick remembered when seeing Marigot for the first time being surprised by how simple and quiet everything was. Few automobiles other than Father LaBourne's car were on the roads. The exception seemed to be beat-up buses and old tap tap trucks. He didn't see any motorbikes zooming up and down the streets. Most people he saw were walking. There were no restaurants that Dick could see, and very few businesses—he only saw people selling food from under umbrellas or on small tables made out of salvaged tree branches. And almost no one had electricity—only a few lights shone from the houses or small shacks they passed. Outside, many people, mostly women, cooked over open fires, having made fire pits by stacking rocks

CHAPTER 4: KAT

into a circle on the ground. Father Redori explained that most everyone cooked outside of their homes because they didn't have electricity for electric stoves, and cooking indoors over open flames was too dangerous. There was no way to safely ventilate when cooking inside. Father LaBourne gave Dick a tour of the schools in the churches, showing him how St. Anthony's funds were providing educational support for the children—he had purchased things like desks, pencils, paper, uniforms, chalk, and textbooks. Dick met students and teachers as well.

The next day, they visited churches and homes just outside of Marigot, in some extremely remote areas. Dick got a deeper sense of how people lived in rural Haiti. He saw humble houses made out of bricks with thatched roofs and mud floors. Other houses were made of wood with tin roofs and appeared unstable, almost as though they were ready to crumble in the slightest wind. He saw homes so small that family members took turns sleeping throughout the day and night because the floor was not big enough for everyone to lay down at once. He saw children with muddy faces playing in dirty water, near trash-filled canals. The children wore torn, old clothes and had no shoes. He saw families begging for money and food. He saw people that looked sick and weak, not having enough food to eat, or clean water to drink.

As they continued their routine for the few days of Dick's trip left, Father LaBourne tried to show Dick as much of St. Dominic's Parish as he could. As he attempted to take it all in, absorbing what he was seeing, Dick became overwhelmed by sadness. He knew that Haitians had few options for making better lives for themselves. He knew few jobs were available, and education was hard to come by—school, even for the youngest children, cost money that most families didn't have. He found himself becoming more and more frustrated now that he could see how much was needed in Haiti—much more than he had ever thought.

When it came time for Dick to return home, Father LaBourne drove him back to Port-au-Prince to catch his flight. Dick's short trip had turned into a weeklong visit. Before he left, he told Father LaBourne he would be returning to Marigot. Just as Harry had hoped, Dick had enjoyed his time in Haiti, and he wanted to come back and get a chance to do more to help.

When he got to the airport, Dick was not as intimidated as he had been when he arrived. As he sat waiting for his flight, he thought about the past week—all the wonderful people he had met, and all the tough realities he had encountered. The need in Haiti was greatly evident to Dick at that point, and more real than ever before. He knew that when he got back home, he wanted to tell everyone he could about what he had seen, both the good and the bad. He wanted to tell people about the difficulties Haitians faced every day, but he also wanted to talk about how beautiful the country was and how kind the Haitians were, how much they had made Dick feel welcomed. He wanted to tell everyone about how strong the Haitians were, and appreciative of everything they had in their lives, even if it was very little.

He didn't know it at the time, but Dick wouldn't have the opportunity to work with Father Redori again. Father Redori had many of his own responsibilities in his parish to attend to, and he would not be available to translate for Dick when he returned the next year. They would not cross paths again in Haiti, but the relationship had still been an important one—it had given Dick a feeling of friendship with a Haitian for the first time. Even though Dick couldn't have predicted it then, Father Redori would

CHAPTER 4: KAT

be just one of many Haitians that he would come to know well and grow close to along the way.

*

When Dick returned to St. Dominic's Parish the following year, he decided before he left home that his trip would last a week. He would again stay at the rectory at St. Dominic's Church. Since Father Redori would not be there to translate, Father LaBourne designated an interpreter for Dick during his visit—a young Haitian named William Penn who served as an altar boy at the church. He wanted to attend the seminary when he was old enough, and he was trying to make a good impression on Father LaBourne, so he offered to translate for Dick. William Penn's English didn't turn out to be all that great, but it was better than Dick not having an interpreter at all.

Dick packed eagerly for his flight, again bringing donations from the St. Anthony's congregation with him. This time, he was much more prepared for his trip. He knew what to expect when he got to the airport, and he had arranged to have Father LaBourne pick him up in Port-au-Prince, feeling confident that he would be there as planned—and on time.

Father LaBourne picked Dick up shortly after his plane arrived, and they made their way to Marigot. When they arrived at St. Dominic's Church, Dick was welcomed instantly— Lorriane, Father LaBourne's children, and all the Haitian church members he had met the previous year were delighted to see him again. For the Haitians, his return to Haiti not only meant that St. Anthony's Church was still supporting St. Dominic's Parish, but, more importantly, that Dick cared about them enough to come back. It made the Haitians feel as though he was a true friend to them.

It was nice to be greeted so warmly upon returning, but Dick found himself feeling slightly disappointed as well—not much had changed in the year he was gone. Marigot still looked the same as it had when he left—he didn't see any new construction, or new roads. It didn't seem that anyone in town had electricity that hadn't already had it before. It was as if time stood still. It was hard for him to see so little change for the community. Even though he knew the amount of money St. Anthony's was sending was small, and it was only for a specific purpose, he was discouraged thinking about how hard it was going to be to make a lasting difference for the people in Haiti. Any kind of change was going to take a long, long time.

Dick had spent most of his first trip to Marigot observing, trying to get an understanding of the lives of the Haitians he met there. Now that he was more familiar with St. Dominic's Parish, however, he was ready to participate. Starting the next day, he and Father LaBourne spent the week visiting churches. In the morning, they would pick up William Penn and head out to visit a different church each day. They performed Mass, and first communions. Father LaBourne performed weddings and baptisms, and heard confessions. They never stopped moving—it seemed to Dick that they were constantly having Mass. On one occasion, Father LaBourne performed eight weddings in a single day. Dick offered a hand in their activities the best he could, and he enjoyed being a part of it all.

On his trip, Dick also got a chance to learn about Father LaBourne's other projects. Father LaBourne did as much as he could for as many individuals as he could reach—he bought seeds and handed them out, hoping to give Haitians an opportunity to grow food for eating or for selling in the market. He bought livestock for families to raise goats and cattle for

CHAPTER 4: KAT

milk or to use for hauling carts. He even got Lorriane involved. Knowing women might speak more candidly with another woman, he asked Lorriane to spend time talking to ladies at the churches, asking them about their particular concerns. She would then report back so Father LaBourne could try to address their needs.

It was evident to Dick that Father LaBourne cared a great deal about the Haitians he served, and his dedication meant the world to the Haitian people they encountered. Father LaBourne was well respected for his work, and Dick was receiving that same respect. In fact, the Haitians treated Dick like royalty when he visited. He ate well for every meal—it always seemed as though an abundance of food was on the table whenever he sat down to eat. And if Dick needed anything at all, he got it right away, even though he did not ask for much. It was important to Dick that he returned that respect to the Haitians, and he was able to do so for the most part—except in one way, which bothered him greatly. In all the time he was in Marigot, Dick never ate a meal with Father LaBourne's family.

Dick would walk into the kitchen of the rectory when it was time to eat and see only two place settings at a table that could easily host ten people. Father LaBourne would join Dick at the table, and Lorriane would serve them and then leave. Dick could hear Father LaBourne's children in the next room, and, every once in a while, one of them would peek their head around the corner and then disappear just as fast. He didn't have to ask why they ate alone—he knew it was custom for visitors to be served without the family, as a sign of respect toward the guest, and he knew he couldn't do anything about it, so he didn't try to argue against it. But it bothered him because it made him feel privileged and set him apart from the Haitians, which he didn't like, and that feeling stuck with him always.

The end of the week came rapidly for Dick, and when it was time to return home, he was already looking forward to coming back to Haiti the next year. He had enjoyed being able to help Father LaBourne and was especially humbled to have participated in so many intimate celebrations. He had gotten a chance to see more of Haitians' culture and traditions, and it had meant a lot for him to be a part of such important times in their lives like weddings and baptisms. They were all so generous to let him share in the festivities, and it made him feel close to the Haitian people. He loved how they celebrated life and was amazed by their resilience. He was infatuated, and consumed with the idea of returning to Haiti to continue to help the people he had come to care about so much. Just as Harry had wanted for him.

*

In February of 1982, Dick made his third trip to Haiti. This time, Father LaBourne planned to take him to the mountains to visit a chapel in Seguin. Located high above Marigot, Seguin was colder and wetter than the less mountainous regions in the country. Because of the harsher weather, the living conditions were also tougher. Even though Seguin was mostly a farming community, many families only owned small plots of land, not offering them enough space to both grow food for their family and grow food to sell for income, meaning the people of Seguin were very poor.

The road up the mountain to Seguin was treacherous. Made of packed dirt and rocks, it was so narrow that it was almost impossible for vehicles to pass one another. Although the two towns were separated by a distance of only fourteen miles, it

CHAPTER 4: KAT

took more than four hours to drive from Marigot to Seguin. Since the trip took such a long time, Father LaBourne planned to spend the entire weekend at the church. William Penn went with them to translate, and Lorriane came along to cook and schedule events.

They began the trip up the mountain in the early afternoon. Father LaBourne was driving slowly. Dick sat in the front seat, bouncing up and down as the vehicle crept up the mountainside. He held onto his seat so he didn't hit his head on the roof of the car while he clenched his teeth with each bump. At one point during the trip, Dick looked out of the driver's-side window and saw a Haitian man on a horse approaching the vehicle from behind. The horse was trotting along rather quickly compared to the speed of the car, obviously accustomed to the rough terrain of the road. As the man and his horse passed them, he waved and smiled politely. Dick did the same, in disbelief that a horse was passing a four-wheel-drive vehicle. He started laughing. When Father LaBourne heard Dick's laughter, he began laughing too. And then Lorriane and William Penn joined in, which made Dick laugh even harder. Dick didn't think any of them knew what he thought was funny, but it made the uncomfortable ride easier for them all.

After arriving in Seguin in the early evening, they settled into the church rectory to get some rest for the night. The next day, Father LaBourne heard confessions in the morning and conducted weddings in the afternoon. It was a rainy day in the mountains as usual. As Father LaBourne and Dick stood outside of the church to greet guests as they entered, Dick noticed a bride riding a horse slowly down the muddy path. As she made her way toward the church, the horse slipped, and the bride fell off, landing in the mud and ruining her white wedding dress.

Dick was horrified. But before he could react, the guests who saw her fall started to laugh. The bride even starting giggling as she sat in the mud, the moment of shock from falling off the horse having quickly passed. Dick was baffled, but as he looked around, he seemed to be the only one who was upset. He decided not to worry about the sodden bride, as she got off the ground uninjured and proudly walked into the church with a smile on her face, just as confident on her wedding day as any other bride Dick had seen.

Those longer weekend trips away from St. Dominic's Church like the one in Seguin were also the trips where Dick learned to drink alcohol. It is not that he didn't drink alcohol before. These were just the trips where he *learned* to drink alcohol—more specifically, rum. Father LaBourne was a drinker. He could put it away. Every night after they finished working, he would pull out a bottle of rum and he and Dick would finish it before dinner. Father LaBourne would mix rum with Sprite or juice and then add ice. Dick was always surprised about the ice. He couldn't understand how Father LaBourne was able to get ice in Haiti. He never saw a refrigerator at any place they stayed when they traveled. Finally, one night, he realized Father LaBourne was buying the ice and keeping it out in the yard, buried in a burlap bag so it would stay frozen.

On their second night in Seguin, Dick and Father LaBourne ran out of Sprite for their rum and Sprites, so Father LaBourne sent William Penn out to buy more soda. He came back with grape soda. It didn't seem to bother Father LaBourne a bit to not have Sprite, and he went right ahead and mixed the rum and grape soda, and Dick went along with it. When the rum ran out that night, Father LaBourne looked at Dick.

"What should we do now?" Father LaBourne said, staring at

CHAPTER 4: KAT

an empty glass.

"Well, we could always get some sleep," Dick replied.

"Oh, no, we can't do that. It's too early. You like scotch?"

"I don't know if I like scotch."

Father LaBourne pulled out a bottle of scotch, and that is when Dick learned how to drink scotch—after the rum ran out.

*

Barb went to Marigot with Dick for the first time in 1983. She had the summer off from school, and, with the exception of Martin, all the kids were older and had moved out of the house. Martin was eight years old at the time, and since he was out of school for summer break as well, Dick and Barb brought him along.

It was particularly hot during Barb and Martin's visit. On previous trips, Dick had stayed in a small room in the rectory, but with the additional guests, Father LaBourne moved them to a slightly larger room with four beds and a sink. The room had very little space for them to spread out and only one small window, not allowing for much airflow. They tried in vain to cool themselves at night with a small fan set up in the corner. But even though the accommodations were cramped, Dick was thrilled to have Barb and Martin alongside him in Haiti. He was excited for Barb to get to see St. Dominic's Parish and how St. Anthony's funds were being put to good use. He was looking forward to her seeing how close he and Father LaBourne had become as well. And, of course, he couldn't wait for Barb to get to know the Haitians as he had.

Father LaBourne was also delighted to have Barb and Martin with them. He was eager to show them the parish, especially knowing Barb was involved with raising funds for St. Dominic's

Church back home. Father LaBourne, Dick, Barb, Martin, and William Penn would all pile into Father LaBourne's car to make the rounds each day. As they drove through Marigot, Barb had a lot of questions for Father LaBourne. She asked about the churches and Father LaBourne's responsibilities within them. She asked about the schools and what the children learned. She asked about how Haitian families lived, and what was difficult for them in their day-to-day lives. Barb's interest was sincere, and Father LaBourne was impressed by her. He spoke more than usual with Barb around and answered all of her questions as thoroughly as he could. Dick found that he learned a lot while Barb was in Haiti—she was good at asking detailed questions he had never thought to ask.

Since Father LaBourne wanted to show Barb and Martin a special time, they traveled more than usual, which was fun for everyone. Father LaBourne took them to the Grande Rivière de Jacmel, the same river he and Dick had passed through years earlier on Dick's first trip to Marigot. This time, however, it was the rainy season, so instead of a small stream and endless flat rocks, the river was rushing with water. In fact, the river was so deep that a tap tap bus had gotten stuck while trying to cross to the other side. They all watched from the car as angry passengers leaned out of the windows of the bus, yelling at the driver for getting them into the predicament.

A few days into their trip, Father LaBourne suggested they all visit a nearby town, La Vallée. Dick had never been, so Father LaBourne thought it would be nice to take them all somewhere new. There was a church in La Vallée, and although it wasn't a part of St. Dominic's Parish, the priest was a friend of Father LaBourne's, and he had offered a place for them to stay for the night. La Vallée, like Seguin, was in the mountains and also

CHAPTER 4: KAT

required traveling up a gravely, narrow road to reach. Thankfully, it was much closer than Seguin—it only took an hour and a half to get there by car.

When they arrived in La Vallée in the early afternoon, the road took them right through a busy market in the center of the town. The market was packed with vendors, and Barb wanted to look around at the local fare. Father LaBourne parked the car, and they all got out, making their way down the crowded street. Suddenly, Barb sensed someone walking directly behind her, so close that she could feel the heat of their body against hers. A hand gently touched her shoulder to motion for her to step aside. When she turned to look, she saw a man with an entire severed cow head balanced directly on top of his head, only about six inches from her face. It scared her half to death.

That evening, back at the church, everyone sat down together for dinner in the rectory, hosted by Father LaBourne's friend, the priest. When the meal was ready, a large platter was placed in the middle of the table. Right in the center of the plate was the main course—a whole cow tongue. Dick and Barb knew what it was immediately, but Martin looked amazed, and then puzzled. He poked Barb.

"What is that?" he whispered.

"Beef," Barb responded. Since they were guests, she didn't want him to get turned off by the idea of eating any of the foods that were given to them, and she figured he probably wouldn't know the difference anyway. And he didn't. Martin went ahead and ate the tongue along with everyone else.

A few days later, after returning to Marigot, Father LaBourne told Dick and Barb he needed to go to Port-au-Prince. He had made plans to have dinner with a group of priests the following evening, and he wanted Dick and Barb to come along so he could introduce them. But Father LaBourne explained that although he would like to include Martin, he didn't believe it was a trip for young children. Martin was welcome to stay at the rectory, and Lorriane could watch over him along with Father LaBourne's kids.

Dick and Barb were unsure about leaving Martin behind. They knew he was safe at the rectory in Lorriane's care, but it was Martin's first time in Haiti, so they worried about him being alone without them. Although it seemed like Martin was having a nice time, having made friends with the other children, it made them nervous, and they couldn't decide what to do. Finally, they simply asked Martin how he felt, leaving the decision up to him.

Martin didn't seem bothered by the idea of Dick and Barb being gone for the evening. He enjoyed being at the rectory around other kids his age. Just like Dick had, Martin was learning to communicate with the Haitian children even though they did not speak the same language.

Dick and Barb went to Port-au-Prince with Father LaBourne the next day. By the time they returned from dinner, it was dark outside. They found Martin inside the rectory with the other children, quietly playing a game. He had had a good day, but Dick could tell something was bothering him. He told Dick while they were away, he ate lunch by himself. Just like Dick, Martin had been treated as a guest, and did not eat with Father LaBourne's children, who waited until he was done with his food to have their own lunch. Dick asked him how eating alone had made him feel. He said he didn't like it—it had made him uncomfortable, but he did not protest. Dick explained that it was custom, and they couldn't do anything about it. Martin had been right by not refusing. But he also told Martin he was proud of him, especially at such a young age, because Dick didn't like eating without

CHAPTER 4: KAT

Father LaBourne's family either.

One of the most touching experiences Dick and Barb ever had in Haiti was on that particular trip with Martin. Martin had never gotten chicken pox at home, even after being exposed to them a few times from his siblings and classmates. But he managed to get chicken pox in Haiti with ease. Martin was miserable. Lorriane and some of the other women from the church helped take care of him. Lorraine would wipe his head with a damp cloth and make sure he was as comfortable as it was possible to be while hot and itchy and stuck in bed.

The Haitians were incredibly concerned for Martin. Father LaBourne's children came up to the bedroom to visit him, and, even though he was contagious, they held his hand and gave him hugs to try to make him feel better. Dick and Barb were deeply touched by the willingness of Lorraine and the children to disregard their own well-being to comfort Martin. They were amazed by the level of love and compassion shown to their son. Dick had seen it before in the churches in Marigot, and he had talked about it with Barb. But now Barb was getting to see it for herself.

When it was time for the Hammonds to return home, Father LaBourne once again drove them to the airport in Port-au-Prince. They had all had a lovely time. Even Martin had had a good time despite his illness. But Dick and Barb could tell he was exhausted and ready to return to the comforts of his own bed. As their plane took off down the runway heading south, Martin gazed out the window. Once in the air, the pilot turned the plane around to head north toward Miami. Martin, with his sense of direction confused, became fearful of returning to Haiti in his tired state and screamed loud enough for all the passengers to hear, "Oh, no! We are going the wrong way! We are going back!"

senk

This is my fifth trip to the FOTCOH clinic in Haiti. Each time it seems to hit me during the first few days of clinic just what these people must endure on a daily basis and what they must have to do to get themselves to our clinic.

Young and old alike walk long distances to get to the clinic. There is nobody dropping them at the door or there waiting with a wheelchair. The ground is rocky and uneven and is difficult to navigate, even with good legs, but they come, as there is no other option.

We helped a 90-year-old man down our road this morning. At first he refused my arm to lean on. Earlier he had told another team member he could make it himself but it would just take some time. Young mothers come with babies or children in tow with nothing but a towel to dry themselves and shield their children from the hot Caribbean sun.

We had several sad cases today. A woman who everyone thought was eight months pregnant actually had other issues causing her abdomen to swell. The medical team all discussed her condition, which, as a non-medical volunteer I mostly did not understand.

What I did understand, loud and clear, was this woman would die soon, and there was nothing that could be done for her because of where we are: Haiti.

-Paul, Non-Medical Volunteer
January 2012

CHAPTER 5: SENK

After five years of working with Father LaBourne, Dick began to feel out of place.

When he arrived in Marigot in early 1984, he knew before the trip was over he would need to discuss with Father LaBourne how he felt. He didn't feel he was serving much of a purpose anymore. He enjoyed working with Father LaBourne, and, for a long time, he thought that he was playing an important role. But as the years went by, he knew he could be doing more. He wasn't overworked by any means. In fact, the opposite was true—it came to a point where he felt like not much more than a guest returning to Haiti to eat other people's food—food that Dick thought should have been feeding Haitians who needed it more than he did.

He didn't want to come to Haiti anymore unless Father LaBourne could give him something to do that was worthwhile in a different way—in a more lasting way. He loved being in Haiti and working with the Haitian people, and he wanted to continue to serve them, but he needed to know that he was helping their lives in a more sustained way.

He waited until the last day of his trip to talk to Father LaBourne. Dick assured him that St. Anthony's would continue to send funds to St. Dominic's, but he didn't want to come back to Marigot without a new spark of purpose. He asked Father LaBourne if he had any suggestions of something else he could do. To Dick's surprise, Father LaBourne didn't think for long. He asked if Dick had noticed how many Haitians were sick in St. Dominic's Parish. Dick answered 'yes'—of course he had noticed. He had seen a lot of sick people over the years. Dick had met people that he knew were suffering from malnutrition, diarrhea, and tuberculosis. He saw a lot of people with colds and bad coughs. And to make matters worse, no adequate health care facility existed near Marigot for Haitians to rely on. The closest hospital in the Sud-Est department was the St. Michel Hospital in Jacmel, which was lacking in many ways as a health care facility. It was dilapidated, dusty, and unsanitary, and it did not have proper equipment or medical personnel. And what's more, even in a medical emergency, it was, and is, required to pay for treatment and medications in advance. If a patient needs to stay overnight at the hospital, it is up to family members to bring food—otherwise, the patient will go without eating while in recovery.

"Is there any way you could come back to Haiti with doctors?" Father LaBourne asked Dick.

Dick paused for a moment, not knowing how to respond. He had no experience in the medical field or with medical professionals. He honestly had no idea if it was something he could do. But Dick was in awe of Father LaBourne's suggestion, and he was excited by the possibility of a new venture. He told Father LaBourne he wanted some time to think about his request. He had tough questions to consider if he was going to figure out how to bring doctors to Haiti.

Dick left with no concrete plans to return, but with a new mission in mind.

*

Father LaBourne had given Dick a challenge—a big one. Although he was ready to take on a new task, the request had not been what he was expecting. But despite his reservations, Dick thought this could be exactly what he was looking for—if he could get doctors to come to Haiti with him, he might just be able to help the Haitian people for the long term.

First came the matter of where to start. At home, Dick talked to Barb about the new plan, and she confirmed what he already

CHAPTER 5: SENK

knew—they didn't have any ties to the medical community in Bartonville. They did know of one nurse who worked at a local hospital, however. They had met her through church, and although they didn't know her well, Dick figured it was worth trying to speak with her.

As luck would have it, the nurse knew a resident who had been to Haiti previously with a volunteer medical group, and she offered to put Dick in contact with him. Dick didn't waste any time getting in touch, and, after listening to his plan, the resident agreed to accompany Dick to Haiti. Without much convincing, Dick had secured his first medical volunteer ever.

From then on, Dick dedicated his free time to recruiting volunteers. He talked to anyone who would listen. As a deacon, he went on a weekend retreat with a women's group where he mentioned his need for medical volunteers. From that, two nurses agreed to join him. As word got around that Dick was looking for medical personnel to work with him in Haiti, a second resident agreed to sign up for the trip. During another church-related meeting, Dick recruited a non-medical volunteer, an ex-Marine from Peoria, to help with carrying supplies, cooking, and cleaning.

Although Dick was enthusiastic about the willingness of people to participate, he was also forward with the new volunteers about what to expect in Haiti. He wanted to make sure they understood he couldn't make too many promises. Since he had never done anything like this before, he didn't know exactly how it would work. He knew the team would have a place to stay and cook food. Father LaBourne had offered the parish hall of St. Dominic's Church to host the clinic. Otherwise, Dick didn't know what it would be like for them. He couldn't make any guarantees about the process of treating Haitian patients, or what particular illnesses or injuries they might encounter. They would have to bring all their own supplies, their own medicine, and whatever equipment they might need. They would have to make educated guesses about what to pack—additional supplies would not be available. The team understood they would be limited, but everyone was ready for the challenge.

Once the team had been recruited, it was time to start collecting supplies. Dick and Barb talked to the St. Anthony's congregation about the new medical mission, and church members started bringing in donations. People purchased pain relief medication for the team to take with them to Haiti. They bought bandages and wound dressings to give to Dick. They purchased vitamins and toothbrushes and soap. Dick remembered receiving a donation of five thousand antibiotics from a local doctor, which at the time he thought was a tremendous amount. (He would come to find out that it was not that much at all.) After months of collecting donations, everything that was donated fit into six flight bags.

Deemed the "St. Anthony's Medical Mission," the team in the end consisted of two residents, two nurses, and two non-medical volunteers, including Dick. Dick called Father LaBourne to let him know when they would be arriving in Marigot. Father LaBourne promised to get the word out to the community so the Haitians knew when to come to the parish hall.

The team arrived in Marigot in January 1985. It was exactly one year after Dick had last left Haiti.

*

The team's plan was to be in Haiti for one week and to see as many patients as their limited resources would allow. But just as they arrived in Marigot and began to unpack their supplies,

CHAPTER 5: SENK

they ran into a problem. Father LaBourne told Dick they were required to get permission from the Department of Health to treat people at the clinic. He had only found out the previous day—having never worked with a medical team before, he didn't know a permit was needed. He and Dick left the parish hall to meet with the medical director at the Department of Health in Jacmel. The team waited nervously, wondering if all their efforts preparing were lost.

Fortunately, after only a short wait to see the medical director, Dick and Father LaBourne were granted permission to treat patients. They returned to the parish hall with the newly issued permit and told the team the good news—they would be allowed to start seeing patients the next morning. They had only lost one day. Although it was a minor setback, it made for an important lesson learned for future trips, and it was the beginning of the established relationship between Dick and the Department of Health—each time he was to return to Haiti, for many years to come, he was obligated to ask for a new permit.

The team woke up the next morning anxious to get to work. They starting setting up the clinic in the parish hall, which wasn't too difficult considering the small amount of supplies they had. They used wooden benches from the church to create a waiting area and placed boards on top of sawhorses to make exam tables. Since the parish hall did not have separate rooms, the team pinned sheets to strings that were hung up across the hall, creating exam rooms to give patients a small amount of privacy. Dick had arranged for William Penn to translate for the team. Since he couldn't translate for everyone by himself, he recruited his brother, Churchill Penn, as well as two other local Haitian men to work with the medical team so that each volunteer had an interpreter alongside them.

Dick was looking forward to the day too—but his excitement was mixed with trepidation. Though he was confident he had assembled a capable team, he was less sure of his own ability to oversee the operations of a medical clinic. Adding to Dick's anxiety was the realization that news travels fast in Haiti, and the number of Haitians that showed up to the clinic was astounding. Father LaBourne had more than gotten the word out. When the team was ready, Dick opened the doors to the front of the parish hall, and he saw hundreds of people eagerly waiting outside, crammed against the walls of the building, all trying to get into the parish hall at once. Taken aback by what he saw, Dick reflexively slammed the doors shut. He had not anticipated a large crowd at all. He suddenly realized that the logistics for the clinic were not going to cut it with the number of people that had shown up. How was he going to decide who came in and who stayed outside? How was he going to determine who should be seen and who shouldn't? He was starting to panic. He knew he had to figure something out, and fast.

Dick came up with a plan. The parish hall didn't have just one set of doors—the building had six sets of doors surrounding all four sides. He started by opening one set of doors and choosing which patients would come in first. He then closed those doors, and gave the medical team some time to see the patients that had been brought in. While the doors were closed, people pressed tightly against them, waiting for them to open again. But Dick didn't open the same door twice. He opened a different set of doors, and found a much smaller group of people waiting. As he moved around from one set of doors to another, no one knew which doors to crowd around, giving Dick a chance to pull in a few people at a time before quickly shutting the doors again.

The clinic ran slowly, and was not terribly efficient at first.

CHAPTER 5: SENK

The supplies the team had so diligently collected for the trip turned out to be not nearly adequate. They had no way of testing patients, so it was difficult to treat anyone unless the ailment was obvious, like a visible injury. Otherwise, if a patient didn't know exactly what was wrong or how to describe their condition, they could not be treated. Because of limited equipment, medications, and medical supplies, the team spent most of the week taking care of colds and treating minor wounds. They were able to do suturing and provide vitamins, and they could hand out pain relievers and prescribe antibiotics. But they were unable to treat diabetes, or to treat hypertension or asthma—conditions that they were seeing a lot of. Medically speaking, everything the team treated was simple. They could do so little relative to how many people needed treatment, which discouraged Dick greatly. By the end of the week, the team had seen just over five hundred patients. The medical mission overall had been trying—a test in itself.

Dick was frustrated. The first clinic had been incredibly hard for him. So many people were in need that it was difficult to feel as though they were doing any good. But he had seen that the team had been able to provide some treatments for the patients throughout the week and that gave him the confidence not to give up. He left Haiti knowing he had to go home and grow the team, and bring more medications next time. He felt that the only other option was to let the medical missions die. And Dick wanted to grow. He would take what he learned and put it into use for planning for the next year. He had faith that he could make it work better, and he was determined to improve the medical team's operations before returning to Haiti.

*

Once Dick got back home, he went straight to work expanding the medical mission—this time, with a better understanding of how to prepare. He worked to collect medical supplies and medications for the following year. Items that weren't donated to Dick that he knew the team would need, like additional bandages, gauze, tape, rubbing alcohol, swabs, and thermometers, he and Barb raised money to purchase. Dick recruited a few new volunteers, and some of the members of the first team signed up to return. By the time they were ready to leave for Marigot, one year after his first trip, Dick's team had grown from six to eight members.

The second medical mission team arrived in Haiti in January 1986. As the volunteers worked to convert the parish hall into a medical clinic, Dick went to the Department of Health to get a permit. Although they had collected a much larger amount of supplies than the previous year, once the team was set up and prepared to see patients, they found that all the medications they had brought for the whole week fit onto one single table.

By the time Dick returned with the permit a few hours later, the crowd had already started to gather at the hall, and he could tell immediately that it was even bigger than it had been before. It was amazing. Hundreds of Haitians stood outside waiting for the doors to open, anxious for the opportunity to be seen by a doctor or nurse. Luckily for Dick, he had anticipated the large crowd. On top of hiring interpreters to work with the team, he had also hired a few additional Haitians to guard the doors of the hall so the team would have more privacy. And, hopefully, the added staff would mean that Dick could better manage the flow of the patients coming in and out of the clinic.

As the week went on, Dick and the team became more aware of typical ailments that affected their Haitian patients—scabies,

CHAPTER 5: SENK

worms, hypertension, diabetes, and machete wounds topped the list. The team was better prepared to treat some of the conditions than they had been before. The first year, they did not have medication to treat scabies, but having seen how rampant it was, they brought enough scabies medication to treat every child that was seen at the clinic, which was, in itself, a big process. Back then, in the early 1980s, scabies wasn't treated with a liquid dose of medication—treatment involved washing each child with a special ointment. So that they could wash the children in the parish hall, the team set up baby pools as washing stations.

But some of the ailments the team saw they were not completely prepared to treat. Although they had brought bandages and ointment to care for wounds, no one expected to see as many burn wounds as they did, and many were extremely severe. Because Haitians mostly cook outside over open flames and because the pots of hot water or hot oil for cooking are exposed and low to the ground, they are prone to tipping over, spilling onto those who are cooking or, more often, small children who have wandered too close to the fire. The team also hadn't anticipated seeing so many machete wounds—deep cuts on the body and severed ears and fingers from men working in the fields. Some of the cuts were so old they had healed themselves, leaving permanent and intense scarring.

Dick took notes every chance he could on how to further develop the clinic. He was constantly thinking about what he could do next time to be more prepared. He was gaining knowledge from the medical standpoint, but his biggest struggle was still maintaining control of the crowd. Even with help from additional Haitian staff, he was still having a difficult time regulating the flow of patients. It was no longer a matter of *how* they were entering the building—it was more of an issue deciding *who* entered the building. It was not an option to see everyone who needed to be seen, let alone everyone who wanted to be seen by a doctor. Dick tried his best to choose those who needed help the most first, but so many people fit in that category—the elderly and mothers with their small children, pregnant women, the injured, the sick, those with burn wounds. Those who had been in motorbike accidents, those with machete cuts. Those with chronic illnesses, those who had never seen a doctor in their lives, those who were so ill that even Dick knew a doctor would not be able to help them.

Outside the parish hall walls, it just seemed as though the crowd went on forever and ever.

*

By the time Dick returned to Haiti the next year he was fortunate enough to establish a relationship with a group in Jacmel that could offer him assistance with the clinics—the Missionaries of Charity. The Sisters of the Missionaries of Charity ran a hospice facility. It was a sad place, but a welcoming facility, and the Sisters took care of patients as best as they could. Sometimes Haitians stayed until they died, and sometimes they got better and were well enough to return home.

Dick reached out to the Sisters after a severely malnourished child came to the clinic and the team was unable to help the boy—they simply would not be in Haiti for long enough to treat him properly. Dick thought maybe the Missionaries of Charity could assist him. They agreed to take the boy right away and made sure he was treated properly for malnutrition. From then on, Dick took patients to the Sisters when the medical team couldn't provide for them, something that was incredibly important to him. The Sisters were also kind enough to offer to

CHAPTER 5: SENK

work as translators for the medical team.

Dick loved the Sisters with a passion. He thought they were lovely people, and he was grateful for their willingness to work with him and the team. He would leave St. Dominic's Church early in the morning, before the clinic started, to pick up two or three Sisters and bring them to the parish hall. The Sisters would translate for the day, and then he would take them back home. Whenever the Sisters were in the car with Dick, they all sat in the back seat together, lined up shoulder to shoulder, and they prayed, rosaries tightly clenched in their palms, eyes shut, as the car bounced up and down the road.

Dick owed his relationship with the Sisters to the head nun, Sister Patsy. Sister Patsy was from India and was a deeply spiritual person. Down to earth, she possessed a quiet confidence Dick notice almost immediately. He thought that Sister Patsy was a jewel. He had nothing but the highest praise for her. And for her part, Sister Patsy was impressed with what Dick was doing in Haiti to help the poor. This mutual admiration allowed the pair to grow close quickly. It got to a point where Sister Patsy trusted Dick so much that she told him he didn't even have to call before bringing in sick patients.

When Sister Patsy left Jacmel a few years later, she first relocated to Port-au-Prince to a much larger facility. The new position was more dangerous and taxing on Sister Patsy. Eventually, she went back home to India. The head nun that succeeded her was, unfortunately, not as willing to work with Dick, and she did not allow him to bring patients to the Sisters anymore. Dick's relationship with the Missionaries of Charity dwindled, but Dick never forgot how much they had meant to him under Sister Patsy.

*

Dick found that trying to get the medical teams in and out of the country could sometimes be scary. During the 1980s and into the 1990s, militia forces controlled specific areas of Haiti, and a few times he was worried about the situation he was getting the team into. But nothing compared to the time Dick got an Uzi held to his belly at the airport.

As usual, the team had been stopped while going through customs to have their bags searched when they landed in Port-au-Prince. But this time, customs officers confiscated all of their bags immediately. Dick didn't even know it was happening at first—one of the volunteers came over and told him that all the supply bags had been taken. Dick looked over to see an airport security officer walking away with the team's medications. He became distressed. He ran over to the officer and asked him where he was going. The officer didn't respond—he kept walking. Dick caught up with him again, just as a Haitian military officer intervened by sticking a gun in Dick's gut. Dick threw his hands up in the air and started to back away. He told the officer he understood that he needed to back off, but he had to have those bags. Without the medications, the clinic could not function. The officer said the bags had to be searched more thoroughly. Dick frantically asked when they would be returned. He was told to come back the next day and talk to someone in the customs office across the street from the airport.

Dick was furious about losing a whole day of seeing patients, but nothing could be done. He would have to wait. He made arrangements for the team to stay at a guesthouse in Port-au-Prince. The next morning, he was at the customs office the moment the doors opened. Immediately, he was passed around

CHAPTER 5: SENK

from person to person, from one office to another, until finally a customs officer instructed him to sign a form, acknowledging that he was bringing medications into the country. Dick signed the paper and asked again when he would receive his bags. The customs officer pointed to another office across the hall. He entered the office and was asked to pay a fee for the release of the medications. Dick paid the fee, collected the bags, and left to meet the team. He was livid about the situation, but thankful that they were now on their way, which was what mattered in the end. So many Haitians relied on the team, and Dick couldn't begin to think of letting them down.

*

Martin returned to Haiti with Dick when he was thirteen years old—this time as a medical mission volunteer. Dick and Barb's other children, although supportive of what they were doing, were older and had made lives for themselves that kept them busy with work and family. It wasn't easy for them to take time to travel to Haiti to see what Dick and Barb were so involved with—Barb with her fundraising at home and Dick leading the medical teams. It was nice to have Martin along. Dick was glad he would have an opportunity to see how the clinic was functioning and how different Dick's work in Haiti was since the last time Martin was in the country. Unfortunately, since the trip was not scheduled during a break in school, Barb couldn't leave, but she did let Martin go—under the condition that he would still do his homework while away.

Martin did whatever Dick asked of him, and although he wasn't allowed to get involved with any major medical cases, he did everything the team did, except drink rum, of course. He packed vitamins into bags to be given to patients. He helped prepare food. He also helped set up the clinic each morning and clean up at the end of each day. Martin made new friends with some of the Haitian children who came to the clinic and also got to visit with some of Father LaBourne's children, who he had befriended on that first trip to Haiti. Martin was, and still is, the youngest person to have volunteered with the medical team.

*

One morning just after the team had finished setting up, a woman came to the clinic with her head wrapped in a turban. She said she had been having headaches recently, so Dick brought her in to see a doctor. The doctor removed the turban and found an enormous growth on the side of the woman's head. After examining it, the doctor decided it must be removed—it would be a minor surgery, but an important one for the woman's comfort.

The team weighed their options—they could take her down the road to the St. Michel Hospital, but there was no guarantee that medical personnel would be available to perform the surgery. They could send her to Port-au-Prince, where better medical services were more likely, but it was a long distance from Marigot, which would make it difficult to ensure that the woman was treated properly. It would also be more expensive to send her so far away. Or, a third option was that the medical team could perform the surgery right there at the parish hall.

The team was comfortable handling the procedure itself. They had the supplies and medications to do so, but they had one big problem—it was much too dim inside. The team went outside and looked around the building to see if another location would offer sufficient light and space. Right next to the hall was a cornfield. The field was not densely packed—it was full of

CHAPTER 5: SENK

cornstalks, but the rows had a few feet of space between them. It was an unorthodox option, they knew, but not only would the field offer enough room and sufficient light, but the cornstalks would provide a little privacy.

The volunteers brought out two wooden benches from the hall and set them down side by side in the cornfield. A sheet was laid across the bench, and the woman lay down on top. As the doctor and nurses prepared for surgery, a Haitian interpreter stood close by, fanning the woman to keep flies away. She received local anesthetic and remained awake for the surgery. A few hours later, after the growth had been successfully removed, the doctor wrapped her head. A short rest later, the woman said she felt fine, and she was sent home, with the request that she return one more time before the team left Marigot.

The woman came back to the parish hall a few days later. She was recovering well from the surgery and was able to leave the clinic without her head wrapped in bandages, and without the need to wear a turban. Before the team left Haiti at the end of the week, Dick saw the woman once again, walking down the street in Jacmel. She gave him a big hug, a huge smile spreading across her face. She was elated to no longer need to cover her head, and it was all because of the medical volunteers.

Dick was proud of what the team was able to accomplish—in a few years, they had gone from not being able to do much, to being capable of handling small surgeries and finding ways to treat people that they previously thought not possible. And it was making a big impact on the lives of their patients. Dick was even starting to see returning patients. He felt that meant the Haitians trusted them, and that made him greatly appreciative of the team's efforts and the good work they did.

Dick and Barb knew that they owed everything to the

volunteers. People who were strangers to them were signing up to go out of the country with Dick, and trust him—even though he didn't have a medical background. They were willing to sleep on the floor in sleeping bags, carry their own gear, and pay for their own flights. They agreed to work in an environment with little privacy, not knowing what kind of conditions they would be treating ahead of time or what patients they would see. Every day was a mystery, but the volunteers rarely got frustrated by the unknown. They never seemed to get overwhelmed by how many people needed to be treated—they simply did as much as they could for as many Haitians as time would allow, finding satisfaction in knowing that the work they were doing was truly helping. And, over time, it had become apparent to Dick, without a doubt, that the medical teams were making a difference in Haiti.

*

    Just a few days after the surgery in the cornfield, a Haitian man was brought into the parish hall complaining of chest pains. Dick could tell the moment he saw the man that he was in bad shape—he could not breathe well, he was sweating badly, and he could barely walk. An examination determined he was experiencing congestive heart failure. He urgently needed to be taken to a hospital.
    Father LaBourne was out for the day, which meant the team did not have access to a vehicle to transport the ailing man. Dick asked William Penn to call an ambulance. Calling an ambulance in Haiti is not like calling an ambulance in the United States. In Haiti, ambulance drivers have to be paid in advance, or they will not take a patient with them. Dick told William Penn he would take care of the cost—he just hoped an ambulance was available.

CHAPTER 5: SENK

Not much later, William Penn returned to the parish hall and told Dick there was an ambulance at the hospital and it would arrive soon. In the meantime, the team tried their best to keep the ailing man comfortable. He desperately needed oxygen, but they didn't have any to give him, so they used a piece of cardboard and fanned him to try to give him air.

Almost two hours went by before Dick heard the sound of a van pulling up to the parish hall. He was relieved initially, but when the ambulance drivers did not come inside a few moments later, he was confused. He figured the drivers must have gone to the rectory to check in with the church staff. Dick continued to wait. The drivers still didn't appear. Fed up, he walked up to the rectory to find out what was keeping them. He found the two men sitting down eating in the kitchen. Lorriane was feeding them, and it didn't seem like they were aware of the emergency at hand.

Dick told the men they needed to get to the parish hall urgently—a man was dying. But the drivers did not get up from their chairs. They continued to eat, seeming annoyed by the interruption of their meal. Dick became irate. He walked over and grabbed the back of one of the chairs and pulled it away from the table, forcing the driver to stand up to avoid falling to the floor. He tossed the chair down, and stormed out of the rectory. The drivers now knew Dick was serious, so they followed him, leaving their food behind. The man was on his way to the hospital just a few minutes later.

Two days later, Dick went to visit the man at the hospital to see how he was recovering. When Dick entered the recovery room, instead of seeing someone who was unable to catch his breath, he saw a man who was alert and, though weak, was chatting with his family. When the man saw Dick, his face lit up.

He shook Dick's hand rapidly, grasping it with both his palms. He thanked him over and over. He was so grateful the volunteers had made sure he got to the hospital. Without the medical team's help, the man would not have survived.

Though Dick and the entire team were thankful for the positive outcome, the situation had made everyone, especially Dick, more aware of their naiveté about doing business in Haiti. He realized that just because "ambulance" signaled emergency in the United States, didn't mean it did in Haiti. He felt softer toward the two drivers—just because they were driving the ambulance, didn't mean they were trained to expect an emergency. Dick knew he didn't want another lapse like that. He made up his mind: If he was going to continue to have successful medical missions in Haiti, he'd have to learn to think like a Haitian.

sis

The question, "What brings you to Haiti?" is often used as part of the team's first day at the clinic. Many tell stories of being invited by a friend who served on a previous team. Some speak of always wanting to serve in a foreign country. Others tell of wanting to give back, as they reflect on all they have been given.

Those who are on a FOTCOH team for the first time are nervous but eager for the adventure, and ready to get to work, not knowing what to expect. Those returning for their second or third trip are more relaxed as they know what is ahead, anxious to renew friendships and greet the Haitian people. Those who have been here two dozen or more times speak of long-term outcomes, and how much more healthy the local population is than when they made their first trip to the clinic.

On the first day of clinic, the large crowd of Haitians waiting outside the enclosed compound are brought inside and given medical care. It is a long day. The team works hard. And after the day is over, the conversation turns to the content, appreciative attitude of the poor, of a case that sticks in their mind because they were able to help that one in a special, personal way, and of how much we take for granted our access to medical care.

It is then that we realized that we are all in Haiti for the same reason.

-Kathy, Non-Medical Volunteer
September 2013

CHAPTER 6: SIS

In 1989, Dick decided it was time to scope out other locations for the clinic outside of the parish hall. The clinics had been going well, but Father LaBourne had been transferred to another parish in Cayes-Jacmel, not far from Marigot, and he was no longer the priest overseeing St. Dominic's Church. Although Father LaBourne had not been around for the clinics very often, having a busy schedule of his own, he had been making some of the arrangements for the team, and without him, and Lorriane, it just wasn't the same. On top of that, the priest who replaced Father LaBourne didn't seem to like the way Dick handled things, and he absolutely didn't want to listen to what Dick had to say. After only one clinic was held at St. Dominic's without Father LaBourne, Dick left Haiti knowing he would bring a team back the following year, but without knowing where they would be working.

Moving out of St. Dominic's would mean big changes to Dick's role and responsibilities. In order to find a new location to host the clinic, Dick needed to arrive in Haiti *before* the medical team to make preparations. This meant he would no longer be traveling with the team, ensuring they made it safely into the country. It also meant that he couldn't guarantee a comparable living space or accommodations for sleeping, eating, and working. Returning volunteers had grown used to working in the parish hall, and they were familiar with the rectory at St. Dominic's, and Dick didn't know what the next place would have to offer. He was unsure of how he was going to make the move work, but he was sure of one thing—he did not want the medical team to disappear completely from St. Dominic's Parish. It was important to him that the team stay close so the same patients they had been treating for years could still expect to receive medical care. Dick figured since he wasn't going to go too far, it couldn't be too hard to find a new location. Or so he thought.

*

When Dick flew into Haiti the next year, he arrived one week ahead of the volunteers. He figured it would give him plenty of time to find a place to host the clinic, find housing, and get the word out to the community where the team would be working.

He checked into the Hotel Cyvadier, one of the few hotels near Jacmel at the time. Located between Jacmel and Marigot, the hotel was a perfect central location for Dick to stay while he made plans for the upcoming clinic. It had small bungalows for guests, as well as a restaurant and bar. He liked the hotel immediately—the staff was friendly and welcoming. He often saw the owner sitting and chatting with visitors, making sure they were comfortable. The hotel also had access to a small public beach. The grounds were well kept, and the hotel had a large terrace where Dick could sit looking out over the water. The view was stunning, and served as a reminder that Haiti could compete with any Caribbean nation as an exquisite tourist destination.

Since Dick had traveled to Seguin with Father LaBourne previously, he thought it would be a good location to host the clinic. Even though he knew how treacherous the road to Seguin was, and what a long journey it was to get there, he had strong feelings about hosting the clinic in the mountains. The people in Seguin were especially bad off, and it wasn't likely that any doctors were traveling to their poor community.

Dick made the drive up the mountain in a rental car he had gotten at the Port-au-Prince airport. He had made plans to meet with a pastor at the church in Seguin, whom he knew from his work with Father LaBourne. After their meeting, the pastor gave Dick permission to use a small government building in

CHAPTER 6: SIS

town to host the clinic. He took Dick to see the structure. It was not large, but it did have a separate reception area and a room that could be used for exams, giving the patients some much needed privacy. The team would be able to sleep at the church, where they would also be able to use the kitchen to cook. It was adequate, and Dick was satisfied that he had secured a decent location for the team.

Dick returned to the hotel. He was glad that plans for the clinic were falling so easily into place. He looked forward to the medical team's arrival, satisfied that the first clinic outside St. Dominic's Church was poised to be a successful one. Relaxing in his room in the Hotel Cyvadier that night, he couldn't have dreamed the clinic in Seguin would turn out to be something he never, ever, wanted to repeat.

Right from the beginning, having the team in Seguin posed a whole new set of logistical problems. When the volunteers arrived in Haiti, Dick met them in Port-au-Prince. Instead of having a flight booked to Jacmel, Dick and the team would be driving to Seguin—it wasn't possible to get everyone and the supplies up the mountain any other way. Because they had to go by car, it took them eight hours to get from the airport in Port-au-Prince to Seguin, which lost them a day of seeing patients just with travel.

The team had also arrived with more supplies than usual—not only did they bring medications, they were also transporting all their own food and cooking equipment up the mountain. Cooking—something that had never been much of a problem at the rectory in Marigot, largely because of Lorriane—was now a major task. When they started to prepare their first meal, they tried to use the gas stove and found that there was no gas. They hadn't known they would have to supply their own. Dick had to hire someone to walk down to Jacmel and buy gas and bring it back. That alone was a whole day's process. And nights were horrible. It was much colder in Seguin than in Marigot, and the team had not brought additional sleeping gear for harsh weather. Dick had never been cold in Haiti except for that trip to Seguin. It was so frigid and uncomfortable, it made it difficult to rest at night.

Dick also had to have an outhouse built on the side of the church to accommodate the team. Before the team arrived, he had hired a few local Haitians to do the job. The men made the outhouse walls by laying wooden slats horizontally, with about six inches between each board. When a volunteer would use the outhouse at night, a flashlight was necessary. With the flashlight turned on, light shined brightly between the spaces in the boards, exposing the use of the outhouse to anyone in sight. If the outhouse was being used during the day, it was likely that a Haitian child would walk by and notice someone using the facility. The children would grab onto a board an arm's length above their head, and then hang down off the side, curiously peering in between the slats. From inside, only little sets of fingers and two eyes showed through to whomever was occupying the outhouse at the time. Needless to say, it was not very private.

Before the clinic had gotten underway, Dick had gone ahead and made arrangements for the volunteers to take turns getting a chance to relax. He made reservations at the Hotel Cyvadier for the middle of the workweek, to allow the volunteers to shower and regain their energy. So that they didn't have to completely shut down the clinic, half the team would go down to the hotel one night and return the next day. Then, the other half of the team would go down the mountain and do the same.

CHAPTER 6: SIS

Everybody seemed to enjoy the time off, but even the scheduled break managed to create an issue. The first group to head to the hotel included the two non-medical volunteers who were in charge of cooking—no one else had been in the kitchen. Since the remainder of the team was not used to portioning food for meals, when they made dinner for themselves that evening, they ended up using most of the food, leaving almost nothing for the entire rest of the week. And because Seguin was secluded and did not have markets to replenish food supplies, the team had to make do with few rations.

Back home, many years before, some friends had given Dick a T-shirt with the words "Dick's Last Resort" written across the front. He had worn it to Haiti on this particular trip, and he thought it would be funny to turn the message into a welcome slogan for the volunteers. He had found a large white sheet and wrote the phrase across the fabric and hung it up on the wall inside the clinic at the beginning of the trip. At the time, Dick and the team hadn't given the message much thought beyond a few laughs. But by the end of the week, they realized that the trip had, in fact, felt like a last resort.

*

Thinking back on the clinic in Seguin, the only really positive thing that stuck out in Dick's mind was being able to help one particular young Haitian boy. The boy had tuberculosis. When he came to the clinic, the volunteers knew right away that they could not take care of him and that the best option would be to take the boy to Sister Patsy and the Missionaries of Charity. Knowing that part of the team was leaving that afternoon to go to the Hotel Cyvadier, Dick decided he and the boy would go with the group, stay at the hotel, and then he would take him to the Missionaries of Charity the following day. Unfortunately, the rental car they got for the trip was not in great shape, and as the vehicle slowly made its way down the mountain, the left rear wheel came completely off. Dick was sitting in the back seat when it happened, and he watched the wheel roll by and tumble off the mountainside. The car came to a stop just three feet from the edge of the cliff.

Everyone jumped out. They knew nothing could be done about the missing wheel, so they left the car on the side of the road—figuring out how to get the vehicle moved would have to wait until the team got the rest of the way down the mountain and the sick child was taken care of. The poor boy didn't even have enough energy to walk. It took a few hours to make the trip, and the team took turns carrying him on their shoulders. Once they got to the hotel, Dick called the rental car agency in Port-au-Prince and requested that they send a replacement vehicle. They did so, and towed the three-wheeled vehicle from the side of the mountain. The next day, Dick took the boy to the Missionaries of Charity, and the team headed back to Seguin.

After they finished up the clinic for the week, and it was time to return to Port-au-Prince, Dick brought the second car back to the rental company. As he was settling up, he noticed on his bill that he was being charged for two missing side-view mirrors—mirrors that vandals had ripped off the abandoned car as it sat on the mountainside, waiting to be towed. Dick did not argue, and paid for the replacement mirrors. At least, he thought to himself, he hadn't been charged for the missing wheel.

Dick later found out from Sister Patsy that the boy with tuberculosis had survived.

*

CHAPTER 6: SIS

Seguin had been difficult, but Dick wasn't going to give up, even though he had to change locations for the clinic—again. He knew he had to be more prepared next time. He had to get consistent help from someone in Haiti. He needed more than just a translator, like William Penn. He needed someone who could find a new building to host the clinic, make plans for housing the volunteers, purchase food and water, as well as hire translators and other Haitian staff. Dick needed someone he could rely on each time he came to Haiti, because there was too much for him to do by himself in the short amount of time before the teams arrived.

That person ending up being a man named Belony. Belony was from Jacmel and knew his way around town. He grew up as a street kid. Small and thin, he was known for being scrappy, a trait he most likely developed to make up for his size. He spoke English fluently, and he always spoke fast. He had a high-pitched voice, and the more excited he got, the higher his voice got. He could stir up excitement just with his presence.

Belony liked capitalizing on his English skills and knowledge of Jacmel to make whatever money he could. He would do anything to make a buck, often on his own terms, but he was also a hard worker. He was a regular at the Hotel Cyvadier, offering himself as a guide or an interpreter for tourists or businessmen who were visiting. Dick met Belony through two journalists who recommended him and vouched for the good work he did. He first worked with Dick as an interpreter for the medical volunteers in Seguin. Dick got to know him better and figured he would be a good resource, despite the fact that he wasn't great at listening to Dick. After offering Belony the job, Dick asked him to find a decent place for the team to work, and Belony jumped right on the task. From then on out, Belony was a fixture at every clinic.

The first place Belony suggested to Dick was in Cap Rouge. Located in the steep sloping mountains directly above Cyvadier, Cap Rouge, like Seguin, was a farming community, where most of the residents grew vegetables and raised livestock. The residents of Cap Rouge were poor, and it was cold and rainy up in the mountains, making the living conditions difficult for the Haitians there. Hosting the clinic in Cap Rouge sounded like a good idea to Dick—he figured if doctors didn't go to Seguin, they probably didn't visit Cap Rouge either. He found out later that Belony hadn't hesitated to forward his own agenda in recommending the location—his girlfriend lived in Cap Rouge. Regardless, they were both about to come across unexpected difficulties. When Dick arrived in Haiti that January, Belony had already secured a building for the team to use. He took Dick up to Cap Rouge to show him. Dick found the building to be adequate, but it was dirty, and in need of some fresh paint—he didn't want patients to see a doctor in a dingy building. He wanted it to feel clean and look as new as possible.

Dick asked Belony to hire a few locals to paint inside the building. When Belony came back a few hours later with a small crew, Dick left careful instructions on how he wanted the building painted, as well as money for the paint to be purchased. He and Belony headed back to the Hotel Cyvadier.

When Dick returned to Cap Rouge a few days later to inspect the building, it hadn't been painted. He was confused. His instructions had been specific—yet nothing had been done, and Dick was not happy about it. He went to see the mayor of Cap Rouge to ask if he knew what was going on. But when Dick approached him, the mayor wanted to talk about something entirely different. He told Dick he wanted to live in the building

CHAPTER 6: SIS

during the clinic so he could make sure he knew what was going on at all times. The mayor wanted to know which Haitians were being treated, and he wanted to have a say in which patients got to see a doctor. Dick told him that was not an option. He would never allow someone else to decide which patients came into the clinic or let another person have control over the security for the building. And he definitely wasn't going to let anyone tell him how to run things. The mayor did not like Dick's answer, and he insisted again that he would be moving into the building for the week. Dick's answer to that was leaving Cap Rouge altogether.

It had been hard for Dick to leave, because it meant the people in Cap Rouge were not going to receive medical care from the team after all, but he had to put his foot down. He had already dealt with a similar situation with Father LaBourne's replacement at St. Dominic's Church. The priest there wanted to interfere with the way the clinic was run, and that had not sat well with Dick, so this was not going to fly either. When he and Belony got back to the hotel, they worked on finding a new building. Within a few days, they were able to secure a house in Cyvadier to host the clinic, and it ended up working quite well for the team. The facility in Cap Rouge never did get painted.

*

Traveling to Haiti before the medical team every year was wearing on Dick. Not only was it more time away from home, and Barb and the kids, but it was also stressful knowing the volunteers and the Haitian patients were dependent on his success. If he wasn't able to secure a place for the clinic, and do it quickly, the team would be out of luck, and so would their Haitian patients. And, it seemed, wherever Dick tried to move the clinic, a problem followed.

After the Cap Rouge incident, Dick and Belony looked for a location closer to Jacmel, deciding to stay out of the mountains. They found a government dispensary in Marigot that was available for rent, and Belony arranged for the team to stay at guesthouses at nearby Ti Moulliage Beach. Ti Moulliage is an alluring white sand beach on the Caribbean coast, with small, privately owned houses stretching the kilometer of the beachfront. The guesthouses are mainly owned by foreigners who have purchased the property and then built small Haitian-style shacks made of local materials, mostly wood and steel, right on the beach. The owners use the guesthouses when they visit Haiti, and the rest of the time they are rented out, with Haitian staff managing the properties.

Ti Millouge worked fine for housing the team, except for one thing—when they arrived to check in, Dick and the team found that the water was not turned on at the guesthouses. Dick asked one of the volunteers to speak with the property manager about the issue, which he did rather quickly. The water was turned on within a few hours. Even though the plumbing at the guesthouses was relatively primitive—the indoor toilets were actually just outhouses inside the buildings—the team was thankful to know they would be able to wash their hands or take a shower after a long day of working at the clinic.

The clinic went well at the dispensary, with the team making the several-mile trip to and from Ti Mioullage on a daily basis, and the week went on without any trouble. Dick was relieved that they had managed to make it through without any major upsets. However, he was in for a surprise. As the team was packing their belongings from the guesthouses, the property manager who turned on the water approached Dick and asked him to settle up with the water bill.

CHAPTER 6: SIS

"Water bill? What water bill?" Dick asked, confused.

The Haitian man insisted on receiving his payment for turning the water on at the guesthouses. Dick was stunned. No one had told him that the rental fees didn't include water and that he would have to pay for it later. He thought it was suspicious that the bill hadn't been mentioned until now. Still, he didn't want to argue and decided to just pay up. Dick asked how much the fee was, and when the property manager told him the amount, it became clear to Dick that he was being taken advantage of. The price the manager was quoting was enormous, and he knew the volunteers couldn't have used that much water—especially without indoor plumbing for the toilets.

The clinic was already operating on a shoestring budget. Dick couldn't afford to go along with the property manager's scheme. Though he didn't feel good about it, he set up a plan to sneak out without the property manager noticing. Dick directed the volunteers to leave in different directions from the guesthouses, so that he could duck out without raising suspicion. He wasn't proud of himself, but he felt he had done the only thing he could at the time. Of course, the team never stayed at those guesthouses again.

The following year, Dick and the team took up residency at a private house near the Hotel Cyvadier. Fortunately, the house was large enough for the team to sleep in and see patients in the same place.

*

One year, and only one year, Dick tried hosting multiple clinics at the same time. The team had grown to around fifteen volunteers, but this particular year, Dick arranged to bring *seventy* people to Haiti. He planned to break the volunteers up into six groups, and work in six different locations for two weeks, instead of their usual one week. The volunteers were staying all over the place—some stayed in guesthouses in Jacmel, a few were at a house near the Hotel Cyvadier, while others where in guesthouses in Marigot.

Dick had intended for the trip to act as training for people who wanted to bring their own medical teams to Haiti. As the word about St. Anthony's Medical Mission spread outside of Bartonville, and outside of Illinois, Dick had more and more people asking how he got started, wanting to do something similar. He was happy to teach others what he had learned. He figured if he could help get more medical teams to Haiti, then more Haitians would benefit.

When Dick made the plan for the multiple clinics, he set up St. Anthony's team at a dispensary in Cyvadier. He spent more of his time there, since it was in the most centralized location. He communicated with the volunteers at the other clinics through radios. Every day, Dick would visit each clinic, making sure the medical teams had what they needed and things were running as intended. In the end, although no major catastrophes occurred, Dick felt that bringing so many people to Haiti had maybe been a foolish thing to do. The clinics had operated just fine, but it had been difficult to answer all the questions that arose as well as deal with individual issues at each site. Not being available to offer advice in person was frustrating for Dick, and it was too hard to manage so much all at once. It was not a job that one person should have been doing on their own. And although the teams had treated patients successfully in the two-week period, Dick himself was spread too thin to feel really useful.

But, despite Dick's personal outlook, it had been a good learning experience for those who wanted to bring their own

CHAPTER 6: SIS

medical teams to Haiti. Some of the groups that went on the trip to learn from Dick did return later with their own teams—some still work in Haiti today. For Dick, the biggest benefit of the multiple clinics was seeing how much it expanded his volunteer group. Several of the volunteers returned with Dick in the following years, and brought more volunteers with them, which was not only helpful, but a lot of fun. Dick loved getting to know the volunteers. Many of them he would have never met in his life if it weren't for the clinics, and he found them delightful to be around. And one of the best parts of having so many wonderful volunteers was the amusing situations they created.

One evening, as the St. Anthony's team was wrapping up for the day, one of the nurses told Dick she had a problem. She had needed to use the bathroom and she didn't have a flashlight, so she borrowed one from another team member. But, while using the outhouse, she dropped the flashlight down the hole. Dick listened to her patiently, trying not to laugh. He knew he needed to keep a straight face since she was so worried about what she was going to do.

Dick paused before making a few suggestions. He first told the nurse she could find a rope and tie it to something, and shimmy down the hole herself to fetch the flashlight. Or, she could hire a Haitian to do the same for her. Or, lastly, he suggested, she could forget about it. Dick pushed for her forgetting about the flashlight, and telling whomever it was she borrowed it from that it was gone forever. Defeated, she took Dick's advice, and left the flashlight in the outhouse. As she walked away, completely frustrated, Dick could no longer hold back his laughter.

A few days later, one of the medical volunteers, another nurse, was flummoxed when a Haitian man brought a patient into the clinic in a wheelbarrow. The nurse checked the patient's vitals as usual, and after the man was wheeled away to see a doctor, she went to consult Dick. She told him that the man's vitals were fine. He didn't seem sick at all. He had even told the nurse he felt good. She was confused. She couldn't understand why the man was in a wheelbarrow. Dick asked her if she checked the man's legs after she checked his vitals. She said no, and asked what was wrong with his legs. Dick, motioning with his hand towards the man, who was by then chatting happily with the doctor, casually pointed out that he was missing a leg. Dick then paused and looked down at the ground, his shoulders shaking as he chuckled. The nurse was speechless.

The next year, Dick went back to hosting only one clinic. Belony found a triplex in Cyvadier, a little closer to the center of Jacmel. The building was called the Sea of Love, and was owned by a man from China who rarely used the building. The Sea of Love had three stories—the top floor housed the men's dorm, the middle floor was for the women's dorm, and the bottom floor was used for the clinic. It had a kitchen, and living space for the volunteers to relax as well. It worked well as a centralized place for patients to visit the clinic, and it was always much easier to have the team living and working in the same building, instead of in different places all over town. It worked well enough that Dick didn't feel he needed to move the team around anymore. The Sea of Love served the team's mission well for many years after.

*

Even with all the issues that arose, Dick had no regrets about moving the clinic from Marigot. He knew that if he hadn't moved, he would have been in constant disagreement with the

CHAPTER 6: SIS

new priest. Dick couldn't have someone trying to run the clinic for him. He worried that if he didn't maintain control, people in the community would be excluded from being seen by a doctor, and he wanted to make sure that all of the Haitians in need of care had an equal chance at being treated. An added positive aspect in moving the clinic was that the team built a stronger reputation with the Haitians they were treating. The team's increased exposure from moving around had helped build trust in the American doctors. The Haitian people were happy with the medical teams and pleased with the medication they were receiving.

Yet even though the clinics were running well, and the teams were seeing more and more patients every year, Dick felt in some ways the work was superficial. The volunteers were treating many returning patients who needed continuous care for conditions like diabetes or hypertension. They saw babies in need of more frequent checkups, and elderly patients living with chronic illnesses. But being in Haiti only once a year meant that the team was not able to provide regular care. They were not able to prescribe enough medication to last until the team returned, further disrupting the continuity of treatment. And it was becoming increasingly difficult for Dick to talk to the Haitian patients about why the team was in Haiti just once a year. Dick started to question it himself, and he began to wonder if he could do things differently so the team could be there more often and give patients the best care that they could provide.

Once again, Dick was reconsidering his efforts in Haiti. He wanted to do something bigger, something with a more lasting impact. He wanted to give the Haitian people something to rely on consistently. While at home, Dick and Barb discussed what they should do next. They were now both in their 50s, and it wasn't too early to start thinking about what they wanted to do when they retired. They knew that, in some capacity, retirement would mean continuing to work with the Haitian people. Before beginning work in Haiti, Dick had always thought he would retire and get some woodworking equipment and start a few small projects, mostly just hobbies. He and Barb had talked about building another house in Peoria. But all that had changed in the last decade.

Neither Dick nor Barb wanted to spend their retirement being stagnant. Barb hadn't even had a chance to get started working in Haiti. She had only ever had the opportunity to fundraise from home and talk about the medical missions. She had yet to be able to participate, and she was ready to do more just as soon as she was done teaching. Dick was worried that if he slowed down after retirement, it would shorten his life. But more than that, they both wanted to do something greater with the rest of their lives, and they knew they wanted to do it in Haiti.

Dick and Barb went back and forth for months, weighing their options. They wanted to continue with the medical missions, but only if the volunteers could see patients throughout the year. And they figured they could only do that if they could find a place the teams could call home—permanently. They wanted to find a building for the team that was for them only, where they could establish themselves formally and not have to pack up all their supplies each time they left Haiti. They wanted more teams to go to Haiti during the year so that patients could receive a regular supply of medication, and the team could track and record patients' progress, and change their treatment plans as necessary.

Dick and Barb knew their idea would require much more of both of them. They would have to spend a lot more time in

CHAPTER 6: SIS

Haiti, as well as recruit more volunteers, hire additional Haitian staff, and find funding for a lot more medications for the added clinics. They would need money to purchase a building, buy medical equipment and beds and kitchen items, and they would need to buy a truck to get the team around.

Dick and Barb knew that if they dedicated themselves fully to their work in Haiti, they would be away from family—kids and grandkids. They would be away from their church and their friends. They would be away from their home and their community. They would miss birthday parties, graduations, weddings, and holiday celebrations. But what they missed at home would be replaced with friends in Haiti, as well as a new place to call home, a new church to attend, and new celebrations in life.

As they deliberated, they also prayed, asking for guidance. They promised God they would do whatever He wanted of them. If it was to dedicate themselves to working in Haiti, they hoped it meant they would be able to provide care on a continuous basis so they could truly help the Haitian people. And with that, they put their faith in devoting more time in Haiti, despite the inherent scarifies and unknown trials. They didn't know where their plan or their prayers were going to lead them exactly, but they did feel strongly that it was time to become independent from St. Anthony's. Dick and Barb wanted to create a separate organization so they could continue to make all their own decisions moving forward. And, more importantly, as they made plans to grow the teams, they wanted to make sure that it was understood that the medical missions were open to people of all religious backgrounds—any volunteer willing was welcome to work alongside them in Haiti.

At home, they got to work establishing a new organization.

They hired a lawyer to file paperwork and talked to the church members and St. Anthony's Medical Mission supporters about their plan to create a distinct entity. The next time Dick went to Haiti, he arrived a week before the team, but this time, the building he was looking for was one to purchase. It only took Dick a few days to realize that a building did not exist near Jacmel that offered everything that was needed to run an efficient clinic. Defeated, he returned home, and talked to Barb about other options. After plenty of discussion, they realized that there was only one way to permanently establish the medical missions they envisioned in Haiti—Dick and Barb were going to have to build a clinic.

sèt

This is my fifth mission with FOTCOH.

I continue to be impressed by the beauty of the country and of the people of Haiti.

I am not a small person who can easily be lost in a crowd and often I see the recognition in the eyes of patients as they approach me. This trip I am working in triage so I take their vital signs and look for any serious conditions that would require immediate treatment. Immediate treatment is a relative term here, of course. In the states, working as a paramedic, I would take many of these patients to the hospital within minutes of onset of their symptoms, but here immediate means they are taken to a provider after they have travelled for hours to get here, then waited in line for their turn.

At home if our prescriptions aren't ready by the time we have the rest of our shopping done, we feel as though we have waiting a long time. Here it takes a day of travel to get medications. If we have side effects to a medication that we don't like, it's OK—there is probably another choice on the shelf. If you don't like the side effects here, there is nothing else.

Many ask me why I spend my money, time, and efforts to come to Haiti. It is easy to understand if you have been here. We are not going to fix Haiti's problems at the clinic. But we will help people while we are here. We will not cure many of them. We will however give many another birthday.

Is it worth the financial hardship imposed by coming here? Just look into the eyes of one of our patients that would not be around today without our help and you will understand.

To those who got nothing under the Christmas tree this year from me, Merry Christmas. This is where the money went.

-Tim, Paramedic
January 2014

CHAPTER 7: SÈT

Friends of the Children of Haiti was officially established in 1991. Barb came up with the name, and both she and Dick thought it was fitting—they felt it was inclusive of not only the children of Haiti, but all of God's children, which reflected their desire to help all Haitian people. Dick continued the regular yearly medical missions at the Sea of Love—now as the Friends of the Children of Haiti Medical Mission Team.

Establishing the new organization in the United States had not been too difficult, but Dick and Barb didn't have any idea how to go about building a clinic in Haiti. Neither of them had a clue about the laws of purchasing property, let alone how to buy building supplies, or the logistics of hiring a construction crew. They didn't know how much it would cost to build a clinic. And, what's more, they didn't actually have the funds to do any of it.

Barb had been busy fundraising for the medical missions for over ten years, but to support this more ambitious project, they would have to come up with new ways to raise larger amounts of money. Barb continued with bake sales and yard sales at St. Anthony's Church as she always had. Both she and Dick talked to anyone and everyone they could about their plan. As they had so many times in the past, they spoke with friends and family about their intentions, as well as church members and volunteers, but this time the idea was grander than ever before.

Mostly people wished Dick and Barb luck when hearing they wanted to build a clinic, but it was hard to tell if anyone actually believed that they could pull off something so big. Some people went a step further and asked them how they planned on making it happen, which they had expected. Dick and Barb were honest, admitting they weren't exactly sure how they were going to do it. But they knew that no matter what, they were going to do everything according to Haitian standards, from working with the government, to hiring Haitian workers. Every part of the process was going to be done the Haitian way.

One day, seemingly out of nowhere, it became apparent that people were not only listening, but they believed in Barb and Dick's plan. On a Saturday afternoon, Barb happened to be absent from a garage sale fundraiser that she almost always participated in. A friend of Barb's who was working the sale called to tell her that someone had left behind a manila envelope. It had "FOTCOH" written on the front and she wasn't sure what it was, but she thought it might be a small contribution of some sort. Barb drove over to her house and together they opened the envelope. Inside they found $6,000 in cash.

*

Barb and Dick never would have guessed that the answer to how they were going to build a clinic would show up in the form of bingo.

Dick was at work one day, talking with an employee about his and Barb's plan, when it was suggested that bingo was a great way to raise funds to get the project off the ground. Hosting bingo was inexpensive, but the return was huge, and people loved to participate because they could end up receiving a big payout if they won. Later that evening, at home, Dick talked with Barb about the prospect of hosting bingo, and they both agreed it sounded like it could work. But since their organization was so new, and not many people in the community were familiar with the name yet, they figured it would be smart to partner with another organization to get people to participate. And naturally, their first thought was to partner with St. Anthony's Church.

Dick and Barb met with the church staff. They explained that with the help of St. Anthony's, they could all make bingo

CHAPTER 7: SÈT

night a popular fundraiser, and both organizations could benefit greatly. Dick and Barb even offered to be in charge of finding volunteers to run bingo night to sweeten the deal. All the money made would be split. St. Anthony's agreed to the new fundraising venture, and, soon after, Dick and Barb found a bingo hall available in Peoria. The owner rented the hall out seven nights a week to seven different groups. Any money brought in after the rental fee was paid, the groups were allowed to keep. Dick and Barb were assigned Saturday nights, where they remained the entire time they hosted bingo.

Barb organized four different volunteer teams, made up mostly of members of the St. Anthony's congregation. Each team took one week at a time, so no one had to work more than once a month. Barb was the exception—she worked bingo every Saturday night. Dick, Barb, and the volunteers ran bingo every week of the year without missing a single week for nine straight years—a total of 468 bingo nights. Bingo was so successful that Dick and Barb raised enough money not only to purchase property in Haiti, but also to pay for the construction of the entire FOTCOH clinic.

*

A person cannot own property in Haiti without being a legal resident. And the legal process in the county is slow at best—Dick was told it would take about two years, and he would have to hire a lawyer in Haiti to file the paperwork for him.

Because it would be such a lengthy process to get his residency, Dick only wanted to become a Haitian resident if he was sure he could find a piece of property he wanted to purchase. With the help of Belony, he began his search for land. As the team continued to work at the Sea of Love each year,

Dick kept up his routine of arriving in Haiti a week early, to give him a chance to check out any property Belony had found. Dick had no real expectations for what he was going to find. He knew he wanted to continue to keep the medical team close to St. Dominic's Parish, so they could continue to treat the same patients as always, but he wasn't looking at a particular location. He wasn't looking for a certain size of land either. Other than being sufficient to build on, he was mostly interested in finding an owner who was willing to offer him a good price.

Since Dick's workload was bigger than ever before, and he knew it would keep growing, he needed additional assistance when he was in Haiti. Belony was fine with day-to-day tasks, but he was usually on his own schedule and would disappear here and there, having a lot of jobs around town. Dick needed someone who could fully dedicate themselves to the clinic plan.

Belony knew of a guy who he thought would be great for the job. His name was Jean Michel Cyprian. Jean Michel was from Jacmel. In his mid-thirties, he was broad-shouldered, with a thick chest and a soft face. Deeply involved with the Mormon Church, he taught kindergarten, and he spoke English well. Jean Michel was enthralled by Dick's plan to build a clinic from the first moment he heard about it—he loved what it would mean for the Haitian people and that made him enthusiastic about working with Dick. Dick was impressed with Jean Michel's interest, and he liked his personality. Jean Michel seemed kind and energetic, and, importantly, he seemed honest, so Dick offered him the position. Once Jean Michel was hired on, he joined Belony in looking for property.

Buying property in Haiti is not easy, even with help from locals like Belony and Jean Michel. Dick knew it was going to be risky and nothing like buying property in the United States.

CHAPTER 7: SÈT

Many foreigners that try to buy land think it happens quickly, or that they can speed it up for themselves, which doesn't always turn out well. Many times, foreigners don't want to miss the opportunity to buy land for a good price. So to make a fast purchase, they put the property in a Haitian citizen's name and then go about getting their own residency. Unfortunately, people get cheated this way if they don't have a contract with their Haitian partner.

Land is also in high demand in and around Jacmel. Jacmel has better security, access to water, and more reliable electricity than many other parts of the country. In more recent years, when the main highway leading in and out of town was paved, an emergence of foreigners came in to buy property, making the availability of land for sale limited. Succession also makes purchasing land in Haiti difficult. Land owned by a person who passes away is divided among their children evenly. Because of this, larger pieces of land don't tend to be owned by one person or even one family, making it hard for a price to be agreed upon. If a piece of property is considerable in size, all of a sudden thirty or forty people could get involved with the sale.

The first time Belony and Jean Michel found a piece of property that was sufficient, the process began straightforwardly enough. They searched out the families who owned the land and got them together to see if they could agree on a sale price. The families came up with a quote, and Jean Michel and Belony relayed it to Dick. The deal sounded good to him, and he accepted. But, then, things got complicated. The families changed their minds (having possibly spoken to other family members living in the United States who suggested they were selling for too little), and suddenly they thought the property was actually worth more. When they came back to Dick with a much higher price, he refused to accept the second quote. And this didn't just happen once—it happened three times.

Dick was incredibly frustrated. Jean Michel and Belony were devoting a lot of time to locating the property owners just to have a deal fall through in the end. And Dick wasn't getting as many offers as he thought he would. The limited options made the laborious bargaining even more tedious. Every time it seemed like the search was moving forward, it fell back again.

Two years into their search, Belony and Jean Michel found a piece of land on the coast between Jacmel and the Hotel Cyvadier that seemed promising. The property was around 50 Haitian acres in size, or roughly sixteen US acres. Every bit of the property was completely covered in rocks, trees, and overgrown brush. When Dick saw it for the first time, one word came to his mind—jungle. It was such a mess that although the ocean was close enough to the property that he could hear the waves crashing, he couldn't get through the thicket to see it.

Three Haitians families owned the piece of land. Belony and Jean Michel worked to get the families to communicate with one another regarding the sale. It took a few weeks, but they finally came up with a price. Even before Dick heard it, he told Belony and Jean Michel to let them know that if he accepted the price, it would be the only price that he would consider, no exceptions. The families understood. They quoted 39,000 US dollars. Dick thought it was fair, and agreed to purchase the property. He had few feelings about the piece of land at first—he was simply satisfied that the sale had required the least amount of negotiating.

Because of the success of bingo, Dick and Barb had the money in place to buy the property. The search was finally over. They were ecstatic. But to finalize the purchase, they had to have

CHAPTER 7: SÈT

a Haitian resident sign for it. Dick asked Jean Michel to purchase the property on his behalf, with the understanding that he would sign it back over to Dick when he got his residency. In the time he had been working with Jean Michel, Dick had come to trust him like no other. He knew Jean Michel wouldn't cheat him out of the property. He was one of the most honest men Dick had ever met, and he was personally invested in his job—he wanted to see the clinic completed just as much as Dick did.

And the trust was worth something. Since Dick was not comfortable building on the property until it was in his name, the property sat untouched for two years while Dick waited for the paperwork to be finalized. When Dick finally received his Haitian residency, Jean Michel signed the property into Dick's name immediately. It was now time to start planning the construction of the clinic.

In a strange coincidence, the property Dick bought had been partially owned by Belony's father-in-law, Esperidon. After the clinic was built, Esperidon was hired as the groundskeeper. Dick and Barb even built him a house to live in on the property.

*

Before anything else could be done with the property, the first order of business was to find water, and then dig a well. Belony told Dick he thought there would be water to be found, but there was no way to know ahead of time whether or not this was true. It had been another risky move, but Dick had gone ahead and made the purchase without being sure of a clean water source. And without water, Dick would own one large piece of overgrown land that would become worthless to him. He was nervous, but he had to have faith that there would be water—he and Barb had come too far to not be confident that it would work out.

Belony brought in a water-witcher, a local Haitian man who used a dowsing rod to search for water underground. If he found water on the property, they would not only know that they could officially build on the land, but where the water was would determine where the clinic would be built on the property. The water-witcher dug into the earth slowly, sometimes only digging as little as a foot into the ground with each day. At the end of every workday that he did not find water, Dick got a little more anxious. Finally, after three weeks of digging and thirty-two feet below the surface, he hit water. Dick was overjoyed.

The next day, Belony and Jean Michel hired a small team of Haitian men to dig the water-witcher's hole into a proper well. Without machinery for digging, the well was dug by hand. Dick remembered looking down into the hole and seeing jagged rocks sticking out all over that the workers had to tediously maneuver around. After the men finished the well, the first thing Dick had them do was put a concrete cap on it, to ensure the water would not become contaminated.

After achieving a few significant milestones toward their plan to build a clinic, it was time for Dick to head home. He was going back to Bartonville to finish up his last year of work before retirement. After more than fifteen years of visiting for short periods, Dick would soon be spending most of his time in Haiti.

That year, in 1997, Dick and Barb sold their share of their business to Dick's business partner, and Barb's cousin, George. The following year, on October 14, 1998, Dick retired. Within one week, he left for Haiti. He had just turned sixty-two years old.

*

CHAPTER 7: SÈT

Dick had initially planned to stay at the Hotel Cyvadier whenever he was in Haiti while the clinic was under construction. The hotel was in a great location, just a twenty-minute walk to the property. But Dick often had visitors, like Jean Michel, Belony, or other Haitian workers, come to the hotel to discuss the construction plans, and it always seemed as though they conveniently managed to show up whenever it was time for a meal. Dick didn't like to eat in front of his guests without asking them to join him, and before he knew it, it was getting costly to stay at the hotel.

Dick decided to seek out a different living situation. He had noticed a house that was under construction right behind the Hotel Cyvadier, just outside of the hotel gates. The house belonged to a woman who planned to move in as soon as it was completed—an American named Linda from Indiana, who had come to Haiti to teach. Her house was large, and it was almost exactly the same distance from the hotel to the clinic as Dick had already become accustomed to traveling. After she moved in, Dick introduced himself and asked if he could rent a room. Linda agreed, and although Dick was sacrificing a bit of privacy, the inexpensive rent went a long way in making the construction of the clinic more affordable.

After settling into Linda's house, Dick got busy focusing on the construction plans. But there was one major obstacle. The dirt road that led to the property off the main highway was much too narrow. Houses had been built so tightly clustered against the road, it would be impossible for a large construction truck to turn onto it. The property was too far away to walk material down from the highway—about a kilometer—not to mention most of the material would be much too heavy for anyone to carry. Dick had to have better access—he needed a new road.

Together, Dick, Belony, and Jean Michel surveyed the property and laid out a map of where an ideal road would exist. Off the main highway sat an empty piece of land, perfect for creating a large entrance to a new road, and only about a quarter of a mile from the original road. The entrance was between a small store, owned by a Haitian man named Son Son, and a house. The space between the two buildings was wide enough to allow room for sizable vehicles to enter.

The easy part was deciding where the road should go—the difficult part was going to be finding out who owned the property. Dick guessed since it was a long stretch of land, multiple families would have to get involved. He was nervous that this could be a major setback to construction. Even if Jean Michel and Belony could locate all the property owners, it wasn't guaranteed they would agree on a price to sell.

Belony and Jean Michel got to work locating the owners. Within just a few weeks, a short amount of time considering the undertaking, they had located the twelve families that owned the land. To try to speed up the process this time, instead of waiting to hear a quote, Dick made the first offer. Surprisingly, the families agreed to Dick's offer, with no negotiating, and they were willing to sell right away. And, since he was a resident of Haiti now, he could put the property in his name at signing. Even today, Dick feels exalted recalling how simple purchasing the road was—by far, the easiest part of any of the building process.

*

"Let the Haitians build their own buildings. They know what they are doing. Whatever you do, hire Haitians to do the work." Father LaBourne had uttered those words to Dick long before the possibility of building a clinic in Haiti had entered his mind.

CHAPTER 7: SÈT

When Father LaBourne spoke them, the words had reminded Dick of the men on the plane on his first trip to Marigot. Dick was determined not to be like those men. It was crucial to him that Haitians were actively involved in all aspects of building the clinic, not off to the sidelines eating peanut brittle. Father LaBourne had also taught him that it was important for Americans to pay Haitians fairly for their time and labor—to not just involve them peripherally, but to actually hire them and show them that they were trusted and respected as experts in their own country.

Belony and Jean Michel were in charge of finding a supervisor for the construction crew. Belony recommended a contractor he knew in town who went by the name Boss Ken. Boss Ken had driven a taxi in Port-au-Prince for twenty years before coming to Jacmel. He had no formal training in construction, but he could build things. A loud, self-involved guy, Boss Ken was also known for being quite flamboyant. He wore boisterous, colorful outfits to the construction site—his favorite of which was the combination of a lace top, with a machete hanging off his belt, and an umbrella hat on his head.

When Dick met Boss Ken for the first time, he could tell he was the type of person who did what he wanted and let everyone else take it or leave it. But Dick could also tell he was a man who would get the job done. He was definitely a *boss*, and a boss was what was needed for the project.

During their first meeting, Dick showed Boss Ken the initial plans for the clinic that he had drawn up. Dick asked him how much he thought it would cost to pull it off. Boss Ken laid the plans out on the hood of his car and studied the design. It took him twenty minutes to come back to Dick with an answer.

The number shocked Dick—it was way higher than he had

expected, or thought was fair. Having a sense for Boss Ken's ambition, Dick figured the quote was a combination of Boss Ken not being one hundred percent sure of what the project would cost and also trying to see what he could get. Dick refused the estimate. Boss Ken went back to the car and studied the plans again. Another twenty minutes later, he came back with a different price—half the amount he had originally quoted. Dick agreed to the new price. Boss Ken would be managing the construction of the clinic.

Although Boss Ken's personality was strong, a mutual respect developed between him and Dick, and Dick especially admired the quality of his work. After the clinic was finished, Boss Ken brought his family—his mom, and brothers, and sisters—to see it. He was proud of his work, and should have been. Years later, the clinic he built would withstand the catastrophic 2010 earthquake.

The design for the building was straightforward—it was basically a box, three-stories tall, that allowed for the space needed to run an efficient clinic, and little else. Although the property was vast, Dick had never intended to build a massive structure. He knew it would be easy to go overboard and build something that went on and on. He had to make sure the clinic was manageable. It needed to house upwards of twenty-five volunteers at a time, and Dick and Barb would need their own space to live six months out of the year, or more. The building would need exam rooms, a pharmacy, a laboratory, a kitchen, and living space for the volunteers to spread out and relax.

Dick based the design of the building on what was available for construction materials in Haiti, mostly concrete and iron. At first, he bought all the construction material himself from a local depot in Jacmel. He would place his order, and a worker

CHAPTER 7: SÈT

would create a ticket for him, which would then be filled. An invoice would be given to Dick when the order was completed, and he would pay for the material and load it up to take to the construction site. After some time, the manager at the depot came to trust Dick, and he was able to place his order and then have it delivered, without the wait—he would later receive a bill for the material. Eventually, he was able to send Jean Michel on his behalf.

Dick was learning a lot about the Haitian method of construction—what materials were available, how much they cost, how Haitians made concrete blocks out of stones. But occasions still arose when he would get confused. Like the time he thought rocks cost twenty-eight dollars apiece.

When the construction crew was first getting started, the Haitian workers would collect rocks from the property to break up and mix with water to make cement blocks. The rocks were free because they were already on the land, but Dick would have to pay the men to stack the rocks into piles closer to the construction site.

The first day the workers collected rocks, Dick asked Jean Michel how much the labor was costing him. Jean Michel told Dick the cost was twenty-eight dollars. Dick thought Jean Michel meant the cost for each rock the men collected, not the cost for each pile they created. Dick was stunned. All of a sudden, he felt he had gotten in over his head. He would never be able to afford to build the clinic—the whole building was going to be made of concrete. After seeing the look of panic on Dick's face, Jean Michel corrected his mistake. Dick was relieved, and a little embarrassed, realizing there were still things he didn't quite understand.

Before getting started on the clinic itself, Dick first needed

Boss Ken to have his workers build a depot over the well. The depot was not only intended for protection, but would also serve as a place to store construction material and equipment. No construction would be happening when Dick was out of the country, so it was important that he had a secure storage facility. It took twenty Haitian workers five weeks to build the depot. When the men were done, Dick returned home for a short break—the holidays were coming up, and he was going to spend time with his family. With the road cleared and the depot completed, everything would be ready when Dick came back. The building plans were in place, the crew had been hired, concrete blocks had been made, and iron and steel were on site. When he returned to Haiti, it would finally be time to start building his and Barb's dream—one they had been waiting to get started on for years, and maybe, without even realizing it, for their whole lives.

uit

I was born on a Monday in the city of Kumasi on what I'm sure was a sweltering evening in one of Ghana's most populated cities. My life story, however, has played out in the comfort and privilege of Canada's peaceful borders, yet I was always painfully aware of the people, the language, the food, and the struggle my family left behind.

I decided to become a doctor at a young age. This fall I have had the experience of a lifetime joining an amazing group of volunteers to serve for two weeks at a clinic in Haiti. I could tell you about the poverty in this country, the mothers who are unable to feed their babies, the heart murmurs so loud they can be heard without a stethoscope, or an elderly woman with skin cancer that had completely disfigured the sole of her right foot. I could tell you all this—I suppose I already have—but there are more than enough sad stories that have already been told from Haiti.

So instead I would rather tell you other stories—about the 77-year-old woman with a large growth at the corner of her left eyelid who I referred to our surgeon. When she heard the word "surgeon" she stood up and ran away with fear so quickly the Haitian interpreters laughed, not believing a woman her age could move so fast. I would rather talk about this place where men and women walk boldly in the streets not concerned by the traffic, but, as our Haitian guide comically pointed out, scatter in fear at the first drop of rain. Let me tell you about the parents who walk for miles and wait patiently under the hot sun for hours, sometimes days, so their children can see a doctor. About a people so resilient that even after unimaginable devastation, they still smile.

-Adwoa, MD
November 2013

CHAPTER 8: UIT

Dick returned home for Thanksgiving in 1998. By the New Year, he had once again left for Haiti, this time with a plan of staying for six months. He was anxious to get started building the clinic, knowing the road ahead would be long.

Barb was still teaching, with a few more years ahead of her before her own retirement. Since she and Dick would be apart for a much longer span of time than usual, Dick tried to stay in touch as often as possible while in Haiti, but it was difficult to call home. Not only did cell phone towers not exist in Jacmel, but if he wanted to make a call, he had to drive into town to the phone company. And because he needed to be at the construction site every day, he didn't have time to check in regularly. When he did get a chance, making a call was tedious. Dick would have to tell the operator at the phone company the number to dial, and then he would sit down and wait in front of a row of booths that were lined up against the wall, each with a small seat inside. Eventually, the phones would ring, and the operator would tell him which phone to answer.

Sometimes Barb wouldn't hear from Dick for six weeks at a time. And although she was just fine at home, still working and hosting bingo, it was lonely without him. But Barb knew it was important for him to be there for every part of the construction, even if it meant he was frequently gone—they had a particular vision for a clinic, and it was his responsibility to ensure those standards were met. Dick also wanted to be available in case any problems came up, or if any part of the plans needed to be changed at the last minute. And Barb knew it wouldn't be long before she would retire and join in, right beside him, in Haiti.

The medical teams continued to see patients at the Sea of Love during the construction, and Dick was just as involved in the clinics as ever. When the team arrived that February, it was just a few weeks after the construction crew had gotten started on the foundation for the clinic building. It was hectic for Dick to have so many roles. He spent the majority of his time just traveling back and forth between the two places. But he knew even though he was swamped with his responsibilities, he didn't need to worry—the team was more than capable. So many of the team members were returning volunteers, and they could handle things as Dick bounced around. He made sure the team got to visit the construction site so he could show them the plans and give them an opportunity to imagine the day, in the not too distant future, when they would have the clinic to call home.

The number of construction workers varied from day to day. Anywhere from ten to over seventy men could be working depending on the stage of the construction. On days when Boss Ken needed cement mixed and poured, he would bring in the largest crews. And it took a lot of men to mix so much concrete. Every single cement block was made by the Haitian construction crew and mixed by hand, on site.

One morning while walking the grounds, Dick noticed that a few men were smashing holes into the wall they had just built the day before. He was shocked. He couldn't imagine why they were tearing down a wall they had just finished. But then the men stopped breaking up the wall and started sliding two-by-fours into the holes they had created. They then laid other boards across the ones that had been inserted into the holes. The men were making scaffolding so they could climb up to build the wall higher. After they completed another section of the wall, they removed the boards, and repaired the holes. Dick couldn't stand to see them build this way—it just didn't make sense to him, and it frustrated him to no end. But the workers would just laugh at him and continue working. Eventually, he stopped complaining,

CHAPTER 8: UIT

because their methods were getting the job done. After all, the Haitian construction workers were the ones with the expertise on how to build in Haiti.

*

On most days while the clinic was under construction, it was not very interesting for Dick. Sometimes he did little more than watch the crew work all day long, something that made his extended stretches of time in Haiti tiresome. Building the clinic was a slow process, and, frankly, quite boring. It didn't help that he was alone in the evenings. So when he reconnected with an old friend, Dick welcomed the companionship. The friend's name was Paul, and, like Dick and Barb, he was from Peoria.

Paul had come to Haiti in his sixties, after his wife passed away. By the time he and Dick reconnected, he had been in Haiti for more than 15 years. He was a gynecologist who delivered babies at a hospital near Cité Soleil in Port-au-Prince. Paul had delivered over ten thousand babies and had been very prominent at the hospital before the administration changed and he was told it was time for him to be done. Having worked well past retirement age, he was getting too old, and the new administration felt he was not cut out for the work anymore.

Dick had known Paul in Illinois—he had a medical practice in Peoria, and he was Dick's mother's doctor for a while. Paul had also worked with St. Anthony's Medical Mission at St. Dominic's Church. Dick had recruited him as a medical volunteer, and Paul thought highly of what Dick was accomplishing in Haiti. He was especially excited when he learned, many years after volunteering with the medical team, about Dick's plan to build a clinic.

When Paul lost his position at the hospital, he didn't want to go home to the United States. He had enjoyed his time spent volunteering with Dick, so when he heard Dick was in Haiti, he tracked him down and asked if he could stay with him at Linda's house. Dick agreed, even though Paul couldn't be much help with construction. But Paul loved being in Haiti, and he was happy to simply have a place to be. Most of the time, he just followed Dick around and was content just doing that. Dick didn't mind. He knew Paul didn't want to leave, because he didn't have any reason to go back home.

Dick and Paul would walk over to the clinic every morning, and after a long day of supervising the construction, they would walk back to Linda's together, usually stopping at the local store, Son Son's, on the way. Located on the main highway right at the top of the clinic road, the store is owned by Son Son himself, a serious and quiet Haitian man. He has a kind face, yet rarely smiles—he is usually wary of the blancs, until he gets to know them. But Son Son got to know Paul and Dick from their evening visits, and he welcomed them to stop by whenever they liked. At the time, he only sold a few items at his store. He mainly carried soda, rum, beer, and dry food snacks, along with whatever Madam Son Son, his wife, cooked—chicken, rice and beans, breadfruit, fried plantains, and pork. She cooked under a little lean-to right outside of their house, directly behind the store. The air around the store always had a delicious scent no matter what time of day.

Linda was a religious woman, and she didn't allow beer in her home. Dick and Paul respected her wishes, so their stops at Son Son's were usually to have a beer, or two, or three, each night. The store had a little bar with only two bar stools. It was so cramped and hot inside that Dick and Paul never wanted to sit at the bar, so they would take the two barstools outside to the front of the building where two chairs sat. Sitting in the chairs and

CHAPTER 8: UIT

using the barstools as their individual tables, the pair would talk and drink beer, and smile and wave at the Haitians walking by. Trucks, tap taps, and motorbikes drove up and down the road, and children road bicycles, kicking up dust in the dry heat of the evening. This was the most relaxing part of the day for Dick and Paul, and it was really the only thing to do outside of working or sleeping.

One afternoon while sitting in their usual spot, Dick noticed Son Son's wife stirring something in a large pot under the lean-to. Right below the large pot was a smaller pot on top of a little pile of rocks. Madam Son Son walked away, heading into the house, leaving her food to cook. After a few moments, Dick pointed over to the pots and said, "I'll be damned, Paul, look at that."

"Look at what?" Paul responded, turning his head.

Dick pointed to the pots. They both watched as a chicken jumped up from the ground and landed on the edge of the lower pot. It then jumped up to the edge of the higher pot. And while perched on the larger pot, the chicken pooped into the smaller pot below. Dick and Paul started laughing uncontrollably, holding their bellies and rolling out of their chairs.

And that was about as entertaining as it got for Paul and Dick.

*

Paul stayed with Dick the entire time the clinic was under construction. Their friendship continued, and eventually Paul moved into the completed clinic right along with Dick. He even had his own room. Paul enjoyed being at the clinic and was just as excited as Dick was about the medical teams working in the new building. He would work along with the other volunteers, even though by then he was too old to do much of anything at all—he would scrounge up patients that needed suturing, or he would invent problems, like bandaging scratches that didn't need attention. Eventually, though, Paul's health deteriorated to the point that Dick and Barb began to fear for his well-being. It was a real possibility that Paul could get ill in Haiti, or even pass away, and they didn't know what they would do if that happened. Even though it was going to break his heart, it came time for them to tell Paul he needed to go home. Paul didn't protest. He knew he had become a liability and that it was time for him to leave Haiti. He agreed to go back to Peoria to live out the rest of his life. He passed away within a few years of returning home.

*

Part of Dick's role in Haiti during the construction of the clinic was managing payroll for the crew. He had always paid the Haitian staff that worked during the medical missions, but it was usually only a few translators for one week at a time during the year. Now, Dick was dealing with a large group that needed to be paid on a weekly basis.

It was Jean Michel's responsibility to work with the Haitian bank, which was located in Port-au-Prince. Since it would take most of the day to travel to the bank and back, the first time Dick needed to do payroll, he sent Jean Michel by himself to Port-au-Prince to withdrawal money, with plans of meeting him the next morning.

Early the following day, Dick drove over to Jean Michel's house. He stopped the truck out front and honked the horn. Jean Michel didn't come out of his house. Dick honked again, and he still didn't come out. He laid on the horn and started yelling for him. Finally, the front door opened, and Jean Michel poked his head out.

"I will be right there!" he yelled, as he ducked back into the

CHAPTER 8: UIT

house.

A few minutes later, Jean Michel walked out of the door holding a small cardboard box. Dick noticed as he walked toward the truck that he was struggling badly. When Jean Michel finally reached the truck, Dick asked him what was in the box. As Jean Michel heaved the box up into the front seat, gasping for air, he said it was the money from the bank. Dick couldn't understand why it weighed so much that Jean Michel strained to carry it.

Dick removed the lid. The box was filled with an enormous amount of coins and Haitian two-dollar bills (equivalent to approximately twenty US cents). The bills were wrapped tightly with rubber bands, in stacks of various sizes and shapes. Some of the stacks were wet and stuck together. Jean Michel said it was exactly how the bank had given him the money—a mangled mess of Haitian currency.

Dick had to make payroll that day, and he couldn't take the time to go back to the bank. But he also knew he couldn't give the workers wads of damp bills and handfuls of loose coins. Instead of going to the construction site, Dick drove to Linda's house so he and Jean Michel could try to sort out the money. When they got there, they sat around the kitchen table peeling apart bills and laying them out to dry. After the money dried, it still took hours to organize it all.

Later that afternoon, Dick and Jean Michel took the payroll to Boss Ken to distribute. The workers were not pleased about receiving handfuls of change with their pay, but Jean Michel explained that the bank had no choice—they didn't have anything else to give. Without any notice of the large payroll withdrawal, the bank only had small bills and coins, some in bad shape.

After the incident, Dick knew he couldn't keep doing payroll like that every week. To sort out the problem, he went to the bank with Jean Michel the next day. The teller apologized and told them if she knew in advance how much they needed, she would see that the money was given to them in reasonable condition next time.

Dick never had another issue with the payroll after that, but he did find that the bank wasn't the only thing he was dealing with that led to unexpected situations. Just as banking was different in Haiti, so was getting electricity to the clinic. Although Jacmel had more reliable electricity than Port-au-Prince, the so-called City of Darkness, power was still distributed on a rolling schedule—different parts of the city had electricity at various times of day, and those times rotated, meaning few Haitians had power all day long. Dick needed to make sure the clinic had enough power to operate and that it would be consistent, and he realized early on that he was going to have to figure out how to do that mostly on his own.

Since the property was a kilometer off the main road, no electrical poles were anywhere near where the clinic was being built. Dick found out that it would be his responsibility to purchase the poles and have them installed—the local power company in Jacmel, EDH, did not install poles or electrical wires. In fact, EDH didn't do much more than turn the power on. They didn't even deliver the power bill—Dick would have to go looking for it where it usually ended up at Son Son's. Dick was able to hire an off-duty EDH employee to install the poles and connect the electricity, saving him money, since his only other option would have been to hire a private local company, which would most likely have been expensive. And even with electricity installed, the clinic still required the use of a generator to guarantee the power would stay on throughout the day and night.

For Dick, such challenges weren't as discouraging as they had

CHAPTER 8: UIT

been in the past. Over the years, he had learned to just go with it. It was a different way of doing things than at home, and by now he knew getting things done would be harder if he expected anything to happen like it did in the United States. Dick was learning how to do things the Haitian way, and he was just fine adjusting, because he knew that is what he had to do to make it all work in the end.

*

By the fall of 2000, the clinic was only a few months away from completion. The building was finished and the security wall around the property had been built. All that was left were the final touches. A shipping container had been brought in from Peoria with bedframes, mattresses, kitchen cabinets, countertops, and ceiling fans. The walls inside and outside the building were painted white.

Since the once-overgrown property had been plowed and smoothed out for construction, Dick was looking forward to bringing in plants and trees to beautify the landscape—he pictured the foliage growing tall and providing shade for the medical volunteers and the Haitian patients, as well as offering some additional privacy for the clinic. Thick foliage would also act as security for the goats, chickens, roosters, rabbits, and dogs that wandered the property freely, not belonging to anyone, but welcome all the same.

One morning while the workers were busy planting bushes, Dick noticed a goat was eating one of his new plants. He walked over to the goat and shooed it away. But the goat just turned back around and found another plant to chew on. Dick tried again to get the goat to move on, but it only scurried away for a moment before returning to nip on a different plant's leaves. Fed up, he picked up the goat and tossed it over the six-foot wall. But before he even had a chance to turn around, the goat had jumped back over the wall, so suddenly it was as though it had bounced off a trampoline on the other side. Dick and the Haitian workers couldn't stop laughing at how funny it had looked to see the goat soaring through the air, so Dick just let it stay and continue chomping on his plants.

*

Although the years of planning and construction had not always been interesting, there had been certain times when Dick did get excited. Phases in the construction where he could see how the clinic was starting to come together were especially enjoyable. At those moments, he felt how promising the new possibilities were—how much the clinic was going to provide for the volunteers, and how much more the volunteers would be able to do for the Haitian people.

One particularly special day for Dick was when the construction crew finished the floor of the second level of the clinic. When he was told that the concrete was dry and that he could go upstairs to see how it looked, he was ecstatic. He couldn't wait to see the progress. He entered the empty building, where the rooms on the first floor had been completed (if only barely, since the walls and floors were nothing more than gray concrete). None of the doors or windows had been put in place, but the stairs had been built. Dick started up the stairwell. He could see blue sky above him coming through the hole at the top of the staircase. When he reached the last step, he walked out onto the open floor. The sun hit his face as he squinted in its glaring brightness. He looked around. For the first time, he could see above the tree line—he had never before seen where the

CHAPTER 8: UIT

building was situated on the property. He hadn't known where exactly the clinic was in that part of Cyvadier, in that part of Haiti, in that part of the world.

As he stood there, Dick's mind flashed to a significant vacation he had taken with Barb and the children when the kids were still young—many years before he would ever set foot in Haiti. They had traveled to Nevada with their camper and stopped for the night at a campsite. Dick unhitched the camper from the car, and Barb and the kids got busy unpacking and setting up camp. As they did so, Dick decided to take a little time to himself to think. He got back into the car, and he drove out as far as he could into the desert. When he became tired of driving, he stopped at the side of a small, rocky cliff and hiked a short distance up out to the edge of the cliff and sat down. He looked out over the dusty reds and golds of the desert landscape, and he thought about what he wanted to do in his life. His mind wandered to what God wanted him to do. But instead of just wondering, Dick started a conversation with God. He didn't ask questions while he spoke. He made demands. He told God that if He put him in a place between the mountains and the ocean, then he would do anything that was asked of him. When Dick was done talking, he made his way back down to the car and returned to Barb and the kids, feeling doubtful that he had been heard.

Now, many years later, as Dick stood on the second floor of the clinic, nothing blocked his view and he was able to see his surroundings in every direction. And as he looked out, he saw that in front of him was the ocean, and behind him were the mountains, and, when he looked off to his side, he could see both at the same time, so close that it seemed as though they were touching. The mountains. The ocean. Together.

nèf

As I come to Haiti this May, I come with a little different perspective. My daughter is pregnant, so I am expecting my first grandchild in September. One of the women I saw today at the clinic is also pregnant and due this September. It made me think of the trials of having children in Haiti. As a provider, I see a number of babies brought in by aunts because the mom died in childbirth. I also see some kids that are starving because mothers have to decide which child to feed. My granddaughter will be born in a hospital having had prenatal care. She will be seen by a pediatrician who will monitor her growth and development. We take so much for granted for medical care in the United States. As I care for the patients this trip, I am thankful I can give whatever assistance I can to make these families a little healthier because the clinic is here.

-Steve, MD
May 2015

The Friends of the Children of Haiti clinic opened in January of 2001. There were no doors in some of the doorways inside, and the stair railing had not been installed, but the construction was complete enough to host the medical volunteers. Dick knew he could take care of most of the finishing touches himself, so he didn't worry too much about the last details. He couldn't wait to have the first team ever work in the new clinic, and he was anxious to find out what a difference it was going to make for everyone.

For the first time, the medical team had a place to store medications all year long, which meant they had less to pack when preparing to travel to Haiti. And now that the team had a permanent home, future shipments of some of the medications could go straight to Port-au-Prince to be picked up and taken to the clinic. Packing up at the end of the workweek would be much easier as well. The medical volunteers no longer had to take equipment and supplies back to the United States. The clinic also had multiple exam rooms where the team could examine patients in private.

The volunteers had actual beds, and hot showers, and linens and towels that could be stored at the clinic permanently. A washing machine was available, so the volunteers didn't need to bring as much clothing as they had before. The clinic also had a fully functioning kitchen with plenty of storage, meaning the team did not have to worry about packing cooking supplies, and dry foods could remain in Haiti for the next group.

The changes didn't stop with the accommodations. Changes in how the clinic operated were immense, and immediate. Because the living situation for the volunteers improved drastically, and the new clinic offered amenities that weren't available before, the number of volunteers that signed up

CHAPTER 9: NÈF

increased. More medical professionals were willing to go to Haiti than ever, meaning the teams were able to see more patients. Whereas before the team could treat roughly 150 patients a day with limited resources, now they could handle seeing 250 or more patients in a day.

Managing the flow of the patients became more efficient as well. At the new clinic, the crowd waited outside the property, making it easier for the Haitian staff to bring patients in to see the medical team in an organized manner. A proper shelter had been built so patients could sit on benches in the shade while they waited. For the first time, too, the medical team was able to offer an educational program, something Dick and Barb had wanted for years. Instead of relying solely on interpreters to explain important instructions, now every patient watched an educational video on how to take their medications properly and how to wash their hands. Women received instructions on how to breastfeed. Patients with diabetes received printed material, in Creole, with pictures to show what foods were appropriate to eat to maintain a healthy diet.

Belony was a part of the educational program from the start, working in the new pharmacy. Although Dick was happy to have Belony work with the medical team, now that construction of the clinic was completed, he didn't need Belony's assistance outside of working as an interpreter. It wasn't that he didn't appreciate all that Belony had done over the years, but Belony wasn't great at listening, something that had caused problems from time to time—the worst of which came up during the assembly of the construction crew. Belony had hired his brother-in-law, who didn't do a good job at all. Dick asked Belony to fire him. Belony did, but then he turned around and re-hired him the very next day. After this happened a few times, Dick became fed up, even though he couldn't really blame Belony for his behavior. Belony was out for himself, and Dick knew that was how he needed to be sometimes to get by in Haiti. But the incident strained their relationship. Besides, Dick had already been relying on Jean Michel for most everything he needed help with—running errands, ordering supplies in Jacmel, interpreting, going to the bank—and he had handled all of those roles professionally. Belony hadn't been nearly as involved as he had in years before, so Jean Michel's dedication to his job had really shone through to Dick. He trusted Jean Michel with everything.

Dick told Belony he was always welcome to work at the clinic, but he wouldn't need his help with day-to-day tasks. Belony took it well, although Dick thought he was more hurt than he let on. Belony continued to work in the pharmacy for many years as a translator, explaining to the Haitian patients how to take their medications properly.

*

One of the first patients to visit the new clinic was a man named Jean Mark. Jean Mark had a cast on his leg. He had gone to the hospital a few weeks prior because his leg had been hurting. A cast was put on it, but the pain continued to worsen. When the medical team examined his leg, they saw blood seeping through the cast. They removed it and discovered a serious infection in Jean Mark's calf bone. They feared Jean Mark was either going to lose his leg, or never walk again. The only treatment the team could offer was antibiotics, and they were not sure it would work, given the severity of the infection. On top of that, Jean Mark would be responsible for keeping the infection clean until the next clinic, which was going to be difficult. The team worried about whether he had clean water at home or if he

CHAPTER 9: NÈF

was even well enough to care for his leg properly.

Jean Mark left the clinic after the team cleaned and bandaged his leg. They gave him enough gauze to last for a few weeks and showed him how to care for the infection, as well as provided instructions on taking his antibiotics. Jean Mark went home and did everything he was told. He took care of the infection so well that his leg actually began to improve. Eventually, he was able to walk again, with crutches, and then a cane. Over time, his leg healed enough to where Jean Mark could walk with no assistance at all. It had taken a great deal of determination on his part, and, because of the new clinic, the team was able to keep a record on him so they could properly follow up with him each time he returned. He became one of the first patients to receive continuous care.

Today, Jean Mark still visits the clinic. No longer for his leg, but for regular checkups.

*

During each of the clinics at the new facility, Dick hired between thirty and forty Haitian staff members, a great many more than he had needed before, and each had a particular and important role. Most were local men and women who Jean Michel recruited to work as interpreters. Others were hired to work in the kitchen or to clean inside and outside the clinic. Dick also hired pill counters and a Haitian pharmacy technician. A Haitian worker provided fluoride treatment for children. Dick hired a few Haitians to organize the crowd of patients, and others to purchase soda, water jugs, and cases of beer and transport them to the clinic. Today, the Haitian staff are so in sync with the daily routine of patients coming in to be treated that even the newest volunteers can quickly learn the flow of the clinic by observing the staff as they work.

While all the Haitian staff members are extremely valuable, one of the most significant people that Dick and Barb have ever had come into their lives is a man named Boyer. Apart from Dick and Barb, Andre Gilles Boyer is the person who best knows the inner workings of the clinic. Currently, Boyer serves as the Haitian director of FOTCOH. He is responsible for maintaining the building, organizing repair work, handling the banking, and helping prepare for the medical team's arrival. Boyer also organizes transportation for the teams and picks up medications shipped to Haiti. Over the years, he has been an exceptional resource for Dick and Barb thanks to his connections within the community. Basically, Boyer knows *everyone* in town, and he knows how to get things done.

Boyer was born and raised in Port-au-Prince, in the Pétionville area. Both his parents were from Jacmel, and his extended family still lived in the area, so as a boy, he traveled there frequently. When he finished high school, Boyer moved to Jacmel to look for a job and to study accounting, learning to speak nearly flawless English during his studies.

Boyer first came to the clinic in 2002 because Dick was looking for a driver. In his late twenties at the time, he was a handsome man with boyish good looks. He had a seriousness about him, a sternness to his face, which made him seem almost unapproachable at first. But after meeting him, it was easy to see that he was actually quite social and talkative, as well as charming. He had a flair for style—the first time Dick saw him, he was dressed like he had just stepped out of a men's fashion magazine. Dick would later learn that the Haitians nicknamed him "Catalog," a moniker of which he was incredibly boastful.

Dick recognized Boyer that first time meeting him, although

CHAPTER 9: NÈF

the two had never formally been introduced. Dick knew Boyer's grandmother—she had lived close to the Hotel Cyvadier. Dick remembered seeing her almost daily, because she always sat on her front porch—unless she was sleeping on the porch, which she did frequently as well. When they met to discuss the job, Boyer showed interest in the position, but wasn't set on working at the clinic. At the time, he was attending the police academy to become an officer. He was, however, intrigued by what Dick was doing. Endlessly passionate about his country and his people, Boyer knew that even though the clinic had only been operating for a little more than a year, it was helping the Haitians in Jacmel immensely. Dick was more immediately interested in working with Boyer—he seemed smart, and capable of doing the job. He also sensed Boyer's intrigue by the detailed questions he asked, and Dick was more inclined to hire someone who he felt was passionate about the clinic's mission.

Boyer told Dick about his police training. Dick asked him how much the police force was willing to pay him. He told Dick what a police officer's salary would be in Jacmel. Dick considered the amount, and asked Boyer to give him some time to think about whether he could make a comparable offer. After a week, he came back to Boyer. He told him he couldn't pay him as much as he would make with the police force, but that he thought Boyer should seriously consider his offer nevertheless. Working at the clinic would guarantee that he would be in Jacmel every day, something that police work could not do for him. If he was needed somewhere else, it would be likely he would be sent away from home. And working for Dick would be monumentally less hazardous—police killings, although sporadic, did happen in Haiti.

Boyer listened to Dick's advice and weighed his options. He

kept thinking about how highly he regarded Dick's work—he could tell that Dick was earnest about growing the clinic. After a few weeks of deliberation, Boyer knew he wanted to be a part of the plan. He returned to Dick with his answer.

"You are a good guy, Dick. You are doing a good thing for my country, and I know I can also help if I work with you," he told him.

Dick and Boyer had mutual good feelings about working with one another. Dick could tell that Boyer was well educated, and it wasn't long before he realized he was capable of much more than being a driver. Boyer was enthusiastic about being a part of the clinic because he saw its potential, and he wanted to be involved in expanding the clinic's programs in any way he could.

Over the years, Dick asked very little of Boyer that Boyer didn't at least try to do. He did his best to find ways to solve problems, and he usually came up with a solution regardless of the issue at hand. Whether it was finding someone to repair a broken generator, or locating a mechanic to fix the truck, or picking up a shipment from a distributor in Port-au-Prince while Dick and Barb were out of the country, Boyer was always good at managing on his own, and Dick and Barb appreciated all his efforts.

Boyer's devotion to his job hasn't stopped there. Since he began working at the clinic, Boyer has always taken every opportunity to talk to people in the community about what the clinic has to offer—medicine, dental care, eyeglasses, shoes, nutritional support for malnourished children, toothbrushes, soap. He tells people it is a place to receive treatment and advice regardless of whether they have money. He is the first to tell anyone that the clinic is more than just a medical facility. There is a reason, he reminds them, that the Haitians call it

CHAPTER 9: NÈF

the House of Life.

*

Barb retired in June 2001, when she was sixty-five years old. Shortly after, she started spending most of her time in Haiti, right alongside Dick. She was delighted to finally be at the clinic. Although she loved teaching, Barb had felt left out for so many years. Whenever she and Dick would host parties at home for the volunteers, she never felt like she actually fit in because she had never been on a medical mission trip before. She had only ever had a chance to visit Haiti once during the entire construction of the clinic. But all of that was about to change. Having never seen the completed clinic, now it was time for her to move into her second home.

Even before Barb finished up her teaching career, she and Dick decided what her roles would be in Haiti—the most important being the job of keeping patient records. Barb would be taking care of the new filing system for dossiers, making sure that each team could easily find a returning patient's information. Before Barb started organizing the records, they were kept without much technique, and it made it hard to locate certain ones sometimes. It was a big task, and an invaluable one.

Barb found herself to be naturally good at record keeping, and from the beginning she considered the project her baby. Something that others would have found mundane, she found gratifying. She developed a system that was simple and efficient—she organized bins of records into alphabetical order, with patients who were seen frequently separated from records for patients who did not require continuous care. Like finishing a puzzle, Barb loved getting to the end of each clinic knowing the records were in order for the next team. It wasn't an easy undertaking. The dossiers were handwritten, and Barb had to learn thousands of Haitian names she had never heard before, and how to spell them properly. If patients had similar names, she had to figure out who was who based on other clues—where they lived, or height and weight, or the date they were last at the clinic. But it was a rare occasion that Barb could not find a record that the team was sure was missing.

Along with records, Barb was in charge of shopping for groceries and cooking for the volunteers. At first, she didn't know a thing about Haitian dishes or what to purchase from the market, but she plunged right into the kitchen anyway, learning as fast as she could about what foods were available in Jacmel and what had to be brought from home. She had no idea what to expect from her first shopping trip, and it was a little unnerving for her. The markets were extremely busy, and confusing. To make it easier, Barb brought Boyer along to do the bargaining for her. He could get a better deal as a local than she could, and he could tell her the names of regional vegetables and the dishes they were used in.

In the beginning, Barb had just enough recipes to make the exact number of meals for the number of days the volunteers would be at the clinic, and nothing more. But as she familiarized herself with the markets, she was able to create an extensive shopping list—potatoes, onions, eggs, tomatoes, green peppers, pumpkin, mandarin, pineapple, bananas, spinach, carrots, beets, grapefruit, and fish. She learned to make rice and beans with lobster sauce (*pwa ak diri ak sos oma*), beet salad with pulled pork (*betrav sos salad ak vyann kochon*), fried plantains (*bannann fri*), and polenta. Eventually, her small recipe list grew, and Barb became comfortable enough shopping in Haiti that she didn't feel like she needed help in the store, except maybe to get something off

CHAPTER 9: NÈF

a shelf that was too tall for her to reach. And Barb shopping on her own worked out for the best in the end—she recalled a time when she asked Jean Michel and Boyer to stop by the market and pick up a can of peas while running errands in Port-au-Prince. They came back to the clinic later that day empty-handed. Neither of them could find "canopies" anywhere.

Barb settled into her life in Haiti with ease, even though she hadn't spent nearly as much time there as Dick had. But they made their home at the clinic just as they had back in Bartonville, and they fell into their routine quite effortlessly. They were so glad to finally be together. After spending so much time apart, they were now able to work side by side to continue to grow the clinics.

Over the years, Barb got to know the Haitians just as well as Dick did, and they began to regard Barb in the same way they regarded him—as someone who was there to help, who truly cared for them. Barb loved getting to know the Haitians that worked at the clinic, and everyone that she met in town. She tried her best to learn Creole words so she could communicate niceties and carry on simple conversations when she and Dick were running errands or having dinner at the Hotel Cyvadier. She and Dick went to church with the Haitians on Sundays and participated in their celebrations. She became close with the women who worked in the kitchen and with Boyer, Jean Michel, and all the other Haitian staff, and they all cherished Barb just as much as she cherished them. Now that Dick and Barb both lived in Haiti, the Haitians affectionately started calling them "Mom" and "Dad."

*

Dick and Barb only scheduled one medical team to be in Haiti the first year the clinic was open. But by the second year, they were ready to add another team to the schedule. And this pattern continued until six teams were traveling to Haiti each calendar year. Not only were there more teams coming to Haiti each year, but the amount of time each team was in Haiti grew as well. Instead of treating patients for one week at a time, the volunteers were now scheduled to be at the clinic for two weeks. With teams visiting roughly every two months, with sixty-five to seventy days between each clinic, chronically ill patients could be given enough mediation to last them until the next clinic. Just as Dick and Barb had wanted, the medical teams were finally able to provide patients with continuous care.

    The hike in the number of teams had everything to do with the added volunteers who had been signing up now that the clinic could offer better accommodations than Dick could previously. And since the team functioned more efficiently in the new clinic as well, the volunteers now had more free time, and their overall experience improved. They no longer had to cook their own meals or pack up supplies at the end of the day. Now the team had a few hours each afternoon before dinner was served to walk to the Hotel Cyvadier to swim, or order rum punch or Prestige, a Haitian lager, at the hotel bar. On the way back to the clinic, the team usually stopped at Son Son's for snacks or soda, or more rum. On the weekend, the team finished seeing patients early on Saturdays, leaving the rest of the day to visit artisan shops and galleries in Jacmel. On Sundays, the one full day off from the clinic, after a late breakfast, the team had the option of visiting Bassin Bleu—a famous, and absolutely stunning, waterfall located in the Sud-Est department—or Ti Mioullage Beach. Each weekend night, the team would go to dinner, perhaps at the Hotel Cyvadier or another local hotel, Cap

CHAPTER 9: NÈF

Lamandou Hotel, giving everyone a chance to try the local fare—conch or lobster, grilled fish or goat.

Many of the volunteers never realize the places they visit and the paths they walk are the same places Dick and Barb visited so many times before—Ti Mioullage Beach, where Dick snuck out to avoid a bill, or the walk between the Hotel Cyvadier and the clinic past Linda's house. They pass the old government building that Dick used for one of the first clinics. The trips to Son Son's, where Dick would sit with Paul and drink beer, soaking in the Haitian life. The road they walk down is the same that Father LaBourne drove Dick and Barb down on the way from Jacmel to Marigot while they visited churches so many years before. They walk by the Sea of Love, not knowing the empty building, and so many other places around them, have been a part of Dick and Barb's long journey in Haiti.

*

Jean Michel and Boyer continued to work closely with the medical teams in the early days of the clinic. They would both accompany the team to the beach or to restaurants, and take them to and from the airport in Jacmel. Back then, before it was updated, the Jacmel airport was nothing more than a small building with a short, gravel runway. Between planes taking off and landing, the runway was always overrun by chickens and goats. In those days, it had been Jean Michel's assignment to wait for the air traffic controller to give word that the plane was ready to depart. He would then go out onto the runway to chase off the animals.

Jean Michel and Boyer also traveled quite a bit with Dick and Barb. Sometimes it was because they needed their assistance with things that they could not do on their own, like navigating around the country, purchasing expensive equipment, or translating. Other times, they traveled together because Dick and Barb enjoyed the pair's company and had come to think of them both as dear friends.

On one occasion, their travels took them to the Dominican Republic. The trip would become impressed on each of their memories for the stark difference between Haiti and the Dominican Republic. After purchasing a new FOTCOH truck, Dick and Barb made plans to cross the border to buy a bumper with a guard. Since they could get the bumper cheaper in the Dominican Republic than they could in Haiti, they figured it was worth the trip. Jean Michel and Boyer came along because they both knew Haitians in the Dominican Republic who could help with the purchase.

To travel from Haiti to the Dominican Republic, a permit is required before leaving Haiti. Then, it takes two to three hours to drive to the border. At the border, an entry fee is due, and, as Barb would recall years later, if you don't have change, you won't get any money back. After entering the Dominican Republic, the truck was stopped at seven checkpoints, each with a police presence. And every time, Boyer and Jean Michel had to explain where they were going and what they were doing. It made the trip much longer, and much more exhausting for them all. In the end, Barb decided they would never drive across the border again—it would have been much easier to have flown.

Even though Haiti and the Dominican Republic share the same island, neither Jean Michel nor Boyer had ever crossed the border. Dick and Barb remembered how difficult it was for them to see their neighboring country for the first time. Considering the nations share the same island, the countries are worlds apart from one another. Haiti is stripped of its natural growth, its

CHAPTER 9: NÈF

mountains bare due to deforestation, and its roads dilapidated. The Dominican Republic is green and lush, with an expansive highway system, making traveling much quicker and safer than in Haiti.

As they drove through the pristine, cobbled streets of Santo Domingo, Jean Michel and Boyer were overwhelmed. They looked out the window of the truck, not believing what they were seeing in the capital—the streets were clean, and the historical structures were intact, the roads gleamed with a sense of newness. So many things they saw were not available in Port-au-Prince: fast food restaurants, organized traffic, sidewalks in every direction. People were in the streets with purpose—people that apparently had something to do during the day, somewhere to be, which felt different because in Haiti work wasn't available for so many Haitians. Both Jean Michel and Boyer, usually so talkative, became quiet in the car, their faces solemn as they looked around in astonishment. How could things be so much better in a country that was so close to their own?

*

Boyer and Jean Michel also went to Port-au-Prince with Dick and Barb from time to time to pick up supplies. It was always useful to have them along, but sometimes their actions, especially Jean Michel's, were more amusing than helpful. Still, Dick and Barb wouldn't have traded them as travel partners for anyone else.

Occasionally, they would fly from Jacmel on a small, puddle jumper plane instead of driving to Port-au-Prince. The plane only had enough room for about a dozen passengers and the pilot, and because there were no compartments for personal belongings, the luggage stayed with them in the cabin, loosely secured behind the last row of seats. On one particular trip from Jacmel to Port-au-Prince, the weather was bad and the flight hit intense turbulence—so much so that the few people on the plane became extremely nervous about whether they were going to make it. Barb had experienced similarly terrifying flights often enough that she wasn't concerned about crashing—she figured that she had lived long enough at that point, if she was supposed to die on the plane, then it was meant to be her time. But around her, the other passengers were visibly becoming unwound.

As the storm persisted, the plane shook and rattled uncontrollably. The passengers began to sing hymns as they gripped their knees or the backs of the chairs in front of them. Luggage started to topple out from behind the seats, and a few passengers grabbed onto loose items while trying to brace themselves to keep from falling into the aisle. The woman seated next to Boyer was holding onto his shirt collar so tightly that Barb didn't think the collar would ever become unwrinkled. It seemed as though the turbulence would never stop, and then, out of nowhere, Jean Michel, wide-eyed, said to Dick,

"Hey Boss?"

"What, Jean Michel?" Dick shouted over the roaring of the storm, clenching the armrest of his chair. He could not understand what Jean Michel could possibly need right at that moment.

"Boss, I got a bad feeling about this," he said, as though just having tuned into the situation.

In unison, Barb, Dick, and Boyer yelled, "SHUT UP, JEAN MICHEL!"

*

Sometimes Dick and Barb would stay at the Hotel Montana

CHAPTER 9: NÈF

in Port-au-Prince to catch early flights home the next day. Once, Boyer and Jean Michel stayed at the hotel as well so they could give Dick and Barb a ride to the airport in the morning before returning to Jacmel. Dick had booked a room for himself and Barb and booked a separate room for Jean Michel and Boyer right next door.

After they all checked into their rooms, Jean Michel went to visit Dick and Barb, mostly to see how their room compared to his. He noticed that they had a balcony, and he walked quickly towards it, not realizing a sliding glass door was in his way—he had never seen one before. He hit the glass door hard, falling straight back onto the floor, obviously stunned. Dick tried hard to contain his laughter, knowing Jean Michel may have been embarrassed. Jean Michel stayed on the floor for a moment, trying to figure out what had happened to him.

The next morning, as Dick and Barb were packing up to check out of the hotel, Jean Michel came into their room again, this time with about a dozen rolls of toilet paper filling his arms. Dick was perturbed. He asked Jean Michel what he was doing with all the toilet paper. Jean Michel told him that since they had paid for it, he didn't see why they would leave it behind. Dick, doing a bad job explaining to Jean Michel that it didn't work that way, blurted out, "Jean Michel, you didn't pay for shit! Put it back!"

And that was the end of that.

*

Jean Michel and Boyer also got the chance to visit Dick and Barb in the United States. Dick and Barb couldn't wait to show them their home in Bartonville, as well as introduce them to FOTCOH supporters who had heard so much about them.

They were thrilled to be able to share another part of their lives, outside of Haiti, with Jean Michel and Boyer, and they looked forward to giving others the chance to get to know them as they did.

Jean Michel and Boyer absolutely loved every part of being in the United States. They enjoyed meeting the FOTCOH board members and seeing the volunteers they knew from the clinic. They were also excited to travel through the Midwest. They went from Peoria to Chicago to visit the Sears Tower. As they drove through Illinois, they were fascinated by the vastness of the land. The farms seemed to go on and on. They couldn't fathom the physical size of the state, let alone the whole country. In Chicago, they wanted to visit all the department stores—all the options of the different clothes and shoes and the newness of everything around them had them both in awe. They also loved the food. Dick and Barb took them out to eat at local restaurants. They ate pizza, and fried chicken. Steak was Boyer's favorite. While visiting, both Jean Michel and Boyer talked about Haiti to everyone they could. They talked about the country's natural beauty and encouraged people who had never visited to see it for themselves. Jacmel especially had a lot to offer tourists, they said. They also spoke about the importance of the clinic for the Haitian people, and why they loved the work that they were doing so much.

Bingo night took place while they were in Peoria, so Jean Michel and Boyer also got a chance to attend the weekly fundraiser. They were both looking forward to the game and the crowd that would be there, so Barb took them to the bingo hall early to help set up. Since they knew they would be meeting people they had never met before, both Jean Michel and Boyer wanted to show off a little. They took pains to come across like

CHAPTER 9: NÈF

macho guys, although neither of them was particularly tough. (Of course, they had never needed to do anything out of the ordinary to make themselves seem special—everyone already thought they were special, especially Dick and Barb.) But it became apparent to Barb that Jean Michel and Boyer wanted to feel like big men when at one point, before the game got started, Barb noticed Jean Michel wearing his sunglasses inside the bingo hall, practicing poses against a counter. He was trying out different positions, leaning on his elbows while sticking his hip out and then rotating his body to stick out his rear and rest his chin in his palm, all while keeping his glasses on and his face stern. Barb giggled to herself as she watched him, thinking about how lucky she and Dick were to have the two of them in their lives.

*

In 2006, Jean Michel and his wife purchased some property not too far from the clinic where they planned to build a house. Dick was happy for Jean Michel, although, privately, he was concerned that the building project might distract him from his responsibilities at work—Jean Michel had already been having some health issues that had been keeping him from working on a regular basis for the last few years.

Jean Michel had started having seizures around 2004. Dick and Barb did their best to try to help him, but he wasn't taking his medications properly, even though the clinic was providing them for him. His health continued to worsen, until he was no longer able to keep up with his work. Over time, Dick became more and more reliant on Boyer. And Boyer stepped up to the challenge wholeheartedly—he not only drove for Dick, but he took over all the banking and payroll, and purchasing of supplies—all the jobs that Jean Michel had done previously. Jean Michel continued to work as a translator for the medical teams as best he could, but at times it was difficult for him to even do that.

Then, a few months after Jean Michel started building his house, Dick received a bill for some construction material, and he could not figure out what the bill was—the clinic was already complete, so he didn't know why iron rods and concrete blocks were being ordered. It occurred to him that Jean Michel might be ordering material for his own home, and sending the bill to Dick. Dick hoped that was not the case, but he decided to approach Jean Michel about it.

When Jean Michel showed up for work that day, Dick asked him about the bill. Jean Michel insisted he didn't know what the bill was, but Dick could tell he wasn't being truthful, because Jean Michel never lied to him. Dick began to get angry. He asked Jean Michel again if he knew anything about the bill for the construction material. This time, Jean Michel admitted he had ordered the material. He said that since he didn't have the money to pay for it upfront, he took advantage of Dick's good graces with the supplier and purchased supplies in Dick's name. He said he planned to pay him back, but he had forgotten about the order. Dick wasn't sure whether or not to believe him, but it didn't matter anyway. It was too late—Jean Michel had lied to him, and his trust had been broken.

Dick and Barb were heartbroken. Jean Michel's actions had been a shock—they had been through so much with him and, up to that point, considered him to be one of the most honest men they had ever met. Jean Michel had always been willing to help. He would do most anything that Dick or Barb asked of him, and he had been such a dependable person. And it wasn't just Dick

CHAPTER 9: NÈF

and Barb that felt that way. Jean Michel had the respect of many Haitians around him as well. Dick ended up letting Jean Michel go, with severance pay. Though it was painful, they moved on without Jean Michel in their lives.

*

In 2009, Dick and Barb moved to Ft. Lauderdale, Florida. They were now in their seventies, and it was getting harder to travel the long distance from Illinois to Haiti—the commute usually involved three or four flights, and it was wearing on both of them. From Florida, they could get a direct flight into Port-au-Prince, saving them time and money each trip.

Dick and Barb announced the move to their children, who were all grown and living in various places around the country. Melissa, Matthew, Martin, William, and Michelle all came home to gather their belongings from childhood, as well as divvy up furniture and kitchen items, since Dick and Barb would not be taking much with them. Their new home in Ft. Lauderdale was smaller, and they didn't need much—they took their bedroom set, an end table or two, a coffee table, a bookcase. They kept some wall hangings and lamps as well.

Dick and Barb had been in their house since 1983. Barb had saved almost everything that came into their home while they lived there—the house had plenty of attic space, and it was loaded. She hadn't realized how much they had in it until it was time to downsize. The kids absorbed most of the furniture, but Barb was still having a hard time getting rid of the things the children didn't want, like old holiday decorations. Barb remembered overhearing Martin, thinking she was out of range, saying, "Mom's not looking. Throw it out!" to his siblings. Barb thought it was quite funny. She knew he was right. It was time to move on, and move out.

Dick and Barb put their house up for sale. The summer they moved, the medical team went to Haiti without them and carried on with the clinic as usual. It was the first time Dick had missed a clinic in twenty-five years.

dis

Measuring the success of global health programs and medical relief efforts is multi-faceted and complex to say the least. However, FOTCOH boasts several features, which have certainly contributed to the success of the organization in providing medical care here in Haiti.

First and foremost is trust. It is easy to see that patients here believe in, and appreciate the work being done on their behalf. Although it is sad to see the group of people who camp out for days waiting their turn, it is a testament to the trust the locals have in this organization.

Secondly is the continuity of care the patients receive. Whether it's a diabetic, hypertensive adult, or a malnourished child, they can rest assured their treatment plan will be scrutinized every two months, and monitored for success. The team is as vigilant with their chronic patients as any clinic in the United States.

Third is the organization of the group. Although there are many first timers, the team functions at a high and efficient level, seeing a tremendous amount of patients in a short amount of time. The teamwork is incredible, allowing both acutely ill and chronically unstable patients to be seen in a timely manner.

Finally, is the sense of family you feel when working with this organization. Some of the volunteers have been working with FOTCOH for years, developing not only friendships among themselves, but with the Haitian staff, and the patients. For those of us who are here for the first time, we are welcomed and made to feel right at home.

Like any healthy family, it is continuing to grow and face daily challenges that are real and palpable. However, the commitment to the FOTCOH family by all those involved assures me those challenges will be met for years to come.

-Michael, MD
May 2013

CHAPTER 10: DIS

In the first years after construction on the clinic was complete, Dick sent patients in need of surgery to the far north of Haiti, to a hospital called Hôpital Sacré Coeur, located in Milot. Hôpital Sacré Coeur had a rotating schedule of volunteer doctors who traveled to Haiti to perform surgeries, and Dick was always pleased with how they took care of patients. The hospital was clean and the staff was professional. Whenever Dick made arrangements for a patient to make the journey, he would give them money for food and lodging, and a Haitian staff member would accompany them to Milot to make sure they arrived safely. Milot was far away—the trip from Jacmel took almost two full days, so a stop in Port-au-Prince to stay overnight was necessary.

Dick wanted to be able to help surgery patients at a facility much closer to the clinic. It always made him nervous to send patients such a long distance, even though he knew Hôpital Sacré Coeur was a good facility. But since the medical volunteers weren't responsible for the surgery, Dick wasn't able to follow up with the patients to make sure they were being monitored once they returned from the hospital, and that made him uncomfortable. He wished there was a better way to take care of patients closer to home, and closer to their own families.

Dick found the solution through a volunteer named Garron Lukas. A surgeon from the United States, Garron had a private surgical practice in Champaign, Illinois, for many years. A quiet man, Garron always speaks slowly and calmly, never raising his voice. He is quick with a joke, although always serious in his delivery. Originally from Detroit, Michigan, Garron attended medical school in Florida. Following graduation, he completed his surgical training in San Francisco and then joined the army, where he was assigned to the elite special operations unit known as Delta Force, working mostly on hostage rescue missions. After seven years in the military, Garron left to start his private practice and teach at the University of Illinois.

Garron first visited Haiti in 2003. At the time his wife, Sharon, was a nurse recruiter for a hospital in Champaign, where she met Kay, one of clinic's volunteers. Kay was leading one of the medical teams to Haiti in a few short weeks and she was worried that she might have to cancel the trip entirely—she didn't have a doctor signed up, and without one, according to the clinic's medical guidelines, the team could not treat patients, and all the planning would be for nothing. Sharon mentioned to Kay that her husband was a doctor and said she would ask him if he would be interested in volunteering.

Fortunately for the medical team, Garron had been looking for an opportunity to get involved with an organization just like FOTCOH, and, even though it was short notice, he was willing to go to Haiti. Not only did Garron go with Kay's team, but Sharon joined him as well. Garron enjoyed his first volunteer experience at the clinic, and he continued to volunteer, sometimes returning multiple times in a year. He got to know Dick and Barb well while in Haiti, and over time he became familiar with the specifics of the clinic's medical program.

After a few years of treating patients at the clinic, Garron discussed with Dick the notion of performing surgery on the property. He had seen a good number of patients who were in need of surgery, and since some of the surgeries were minor, he knew he would be able to perform them himself instead of sending the patients all the way to Milot. Dick agreed it was a good idea, and he gave Garron the go ahead to do surgeries on site. And, just like the surgery the team had performed on the woman in the cornfield in the early days of the medical missions, Garron performed his surgeries outside, taking advantage of the

CHAPTER 10: DIS

natural light, on an exam table set up under a tree in the shade, away from the other patients.

After performing a number of successful, simple surgeries, however, Garron knew he wanted to do more for his patients. To do that, he would need to work in an appropriate facility—one that could offer post-surgery care and allow him to take on more serious cases. He was seeing patients with tumors and hernias, and he just wasn't able to do that type of surgery at the clinic. Garron and Dick weighed their options and decided they would look into adding a proper surgery program to the clinic operations.

A few months later, Garron and Dick set out to visit hospitals in Haiti to see how other surgery programs worked—what equipment was being used and what kind of surgeries were being performed. Although an experienced surgeon, Garron didn't know what it would take to meet the requirements for surgery in Haiti—getting an idea of how other hospitals operated was crucial. They visited hospitals and clinics throughout northern Haiti, including rural hospitals. They visited facilities run by both Haitians and foreigners. Although some of the places they saw had decent equipment and sanitation practices, Garron found the standards fairly low—crude, even, compared to the United States. He was confident that he would not only be able to achieve basic standards of care in Haiti, but most likely exceed those standards.

After returning from their travels, Dick and Garron set out to find a location in Jacmel that would be adequate for a surgery program and postoperative monitoring. The first place they visited was St. Michel Hospital, the largest hospital in the Sud-Est department and the one closest to the clinic. Garron found the conditions to be unacceptable. The hospital consisted of multiple dilapidated buildings spread out over a massive piece of land, each building indecipherable from the next and none appearing particularly safe for a patient to enter. Outside the main building, where new patients checked in, a stack of old desks and chairs were piled almost two stories high, crowding the entryway. In the waiting room, dusty old hospital beds and broken office furniture shared the room with patients and their family members. Nothing was clean. The operating room had open windows. The staff was reusing surgical gloves. Garron didn't feel that any safe surgery was taking place there.

After leaving St. Michel, they visited the Dr. Martinez Hospital, located in the heart of Jacmel. A small, private hospital, the Dr. Martinez Hospital was run by Dr. Robert Martinez, a Haitian doctor specializing in obstetrics and gynecology. Dick knew Dr. Martinez—he had volunteered with the early medical missions before the clinic was built, and Dick liked working with him, finding him professional and kind. Dr. Martinez also spoke Creole and some English, which had allowed him to converse freely with the patients and the medical volunteers.

The Dr. Martinez Hospital was close to the clinic as well, and, since St. Michel Hospital was off their list, it became the next best option—just as long as it was up to par. When they arrived, Garron could tell immediately the hospital was in much better condition than St. Michel. The hospital was painted bright blue and pale green, and vibrant, green shrubs surrounded the small parking lot. When Garron and Dick went inside, they found the surgical room on the first floor, and patient rooms on both the first and second floors. The hospital also had a delivery room. All the rooms were sterile, and tidy. The hospital had a small laboratory and a pharmacy, both of which were orderly and sanitary. Garron and Dick were both satisfied with how clean and well maintained the whole hospital was—compared to St. Michel,

CHAPTER 10: DIS

the difference was night and day.

During their visit, Dick and Garron also got a chance to meet with Dr. Martinez and explain their intentions. Dr. Martinez was hopeful about the possibilities of working with Garron. He could offer the space to perform surgery, as well as allow them to keep surgical equipment safely at the hospital. In exchange, FOTCOH would pay a fee per patient to use the facility.

Dick and Garron felt assured that working with Dr. Martinez was the right move. As they headed back to the clinic, they were confident in having taken the first step towards creating the surgery program, yet realistic about how much needed to be done. It would still be a long time before Garron would be ready to perform surgery, even with the space within the hospital secured. He needed proper surgical equipment and a sterilizer, as well as an anesthesia machine. Purchasing these items, all of which were expensive, and getting them into the country would not be a simple task. In all, it would take Garron nearly two years to get the equipment he needed into Haiti to get the surgery program started.

*

Dr. Martinez introduced Garron to Dr. Frantzso Nelson in 2006. When the pair met, Nelson was in his early thirties and had been working with Dr. Martinez for two years. He was a soft-spoken man, known for his kindness and patience. Always seen with a big grin on his face, he never seemed stressed, or fatigued, even though his job at the hospital was demanding.

Nelson was from Jacmel, but he attended medical school in the Dominican Republic. Medical schools are more plentiful in the Dominican Republic than in Haiti—the Haitian government only accepts about one hundred students a year into medical schools in the country, making the application process very competitive. After finishing medical school, Nelson returned to Jacmel to find a job working with a local doctor so he could acquire experience—there was no residency program in Haiti, so it was up to him to get the training he needed to practice medicine on his own. In 2004, he began working with Dr. Martinez. He learned a lot under Dr. Martinez's stewardship and, after a few years, he started his own practice within the hospital, which he still has today. He also runs a free clinic in a slum area of Jacmel.

When Dr. Martinez introduced Garron and Nelson, he suggested that Nelson would make a good assistant once the new surgery program got started. Nelson liked the idea—he knew he could learn a lot from an experienced surgeon like Garron. And Garron agreed that it would be helpful to have someone who lived in Jacmel to work alongside him. That way, he wouldn't have to worry about surgery patients after he left Haiti. If any complications arose when Garron was gone, Nelson would already be at the hospital. To this day, one of Nelson's most important roles in his work with the surgery program is overseeing the post-surgical care of Garron's patients.

Nelson was also able to help Garron in other significant ways. From the beginning, Garron knew he needed an anesthesiologist, someone who was qualified and able to work for a few weeks at a time at the hospital throughout the year. He didn't know many Haitian medical professionals, especially in specialized fields, and without one, the surgery program could not function. Luckily, Nelson knew someone—an anesthesiologist named Dr. Blasey, who lived in Port-au-Prince. At Nelson's persuasion, Dr. Blasey agreed to travel to Jacmel whenever Garron was performing surgery. Without Nelson's recommendation, the surgery program

CHAPTER 10: DIS

might have not gotten off the ground. Over the years, Nelson continued to be an outstanding resource whenever the situation required a specialist, and Garron was endlessly grateful for everything he was able to do to help with the surgery program's success.

Back at home, Garron worked to get surgical supplies collected. Some surgical instruments were donated by the hospital where he had his practice in Illinois, and he was able to secure a grant through a charitable foundation to purchase other items he needed. He also received donations of electrosurgical units and autoclaves from US manufacturers of the instruments. With each trip that Garron made to Haiti to volunteer at the clinic, he would bring surgical equipment with him piece by piece, until he had adequate equipment in place to start the program.

With his team in order, the hospital secured, and the surgery equipment purchased and brought into Jacmel, Garron was finally ready to start performing surgery at the Dr. Martinez Hospital. After years of preparing, he couldn't be more pleased with how the program was turning out, especially with the help of Nelson and Dr. Blasey. When the surgery program officially began in 2007, Garron felt that it was better than most he had seen in Haiti.

*

Nelson not only worked closely with Garron, but was also able to offer the team something invaluable—insight into the lives of Haitians. As the only Haitian doctor that has worked at the clinic on a consistent basis, Nelson continuously helped the volunteers understand how Haitians think about health care, and how their beliefs structure those feelings. Nelson explained that, many times, the way Haitians think about their health is deeply influenced by their practice of Vodou. And although roughly eighty percent of Haitians consider themselves Catholic, and twenty percent consider themselves Protestant, as Barb will contest, *all* Haitians believe in Vodou.

Vodou originated in the 1700s, when African slaves who were brought to Haiti developed their own religion. After being forcefully Christianized upon arriving in the country, slaves who did not want to give up their own religious beliefs and traditions combined aspects of African religious traditions and Catholicism to create Vodou. Those who practice Vodou offer prayers to spirits who are thought to provide protection, healing, and good health. Prayer offerings usually involve various ceremonies and rituals, often with a component of music and dance.

Because of his knowledge of Vodou and Haitian culture, Nelson was especially helpful to the volunteers whenever a patient seemed unresponsive during examinations. Many times, he explained, if a person goes to a Vodou priest to be healed of a health issue, the priest will tell a person what is ailing them without asking any questions about their symptoms. Because of this, Haitians sometimes believe that American doctors should know what is wrong without answering any questions or without being examined. This trust in Vodou traditions can make it difficult for foreign doctors to treat their Haitian patients properly.

According to Nelson, many Haitians don't always want to trust Vodou in every part of their lives, but sometimes they have no other resources for receiving help. When they can't afford to see a doctor, they go to a Vodou priest. Like so many people in the world, they want to believe in something that offers them hope in their day-to-day lives, and trusting in Vodou when their health is at risk is sometimes all they have. But, as Nelson would

CHAPTER 10: DIS

argue, just as Haitians might believe in Catholicism and Vodou at the same time, they also believe in Western medicine and Vodou practices simultaneously.

Nelson also says that since he has worked for the clinic, he has seen Haitians change the way they think about their health. He has seen many Haitians returning to the clinic because they are feeling better. They believe the medications they are receiving are working. He knows they are also talking to their family and friends about the care they are receiving and encouraging them to see a doctor as well. He feels, without a doubt, that the Haitians trust the medical teams, and they trust the clinic.

*

Some of the things Garron has seen while performing surgery are not surprising to him, considering his career, but some things even he could not have anticipated. He had never before had to consider what he would do if a piece of surgical equipment broke, because in the United States it could be fixed. But in Haiti, it wasn't guaranteed that there would be someone who knew how to fix specialized equipment, which meant if something broke, surgery could be held up for an unforeseeable amount of time.

Garron also had to consider whether he would have access to clean water, or whether or not electricity would be available in the hospital, something he normally never would have given a second thought. Initially, he used the city power at the hospital, but electrical surges took a toll on the equipment. It became necessary to start using a generator for all the surgery cases. One day, while Garron was performing surgery on a man who had a large hernia, the room went black. The man's intestines had been sitting out on his abdominal wall at the time. Now, as Nelson hurried out of the operating room to find out what happened,

Garron waited in the dark, holding the man's intestines. Nelson came back and told Garron the generator had run out of gas, and he had to go out to get more. Half an hour went by before Nelson returned and filled the generator. The lights came back on, and they continued with the surgery.

But even though there have been unforeseen circumstances along the way, the surgeries Garron has performed have been incredibly successful. Garron is proud of the record of the surgery program at the Dr. Martinez Hospital, and he is especially proud of Nelson's progress over the years. Although he had little surgical experience at first, Nelson has learned a lot working alongside Garron. When they began working together, Nelson called Garron at home three or four times a month to ask questions. Gradually, those calls became less frequent, as Nelson became more comfortable with his capability to take care of patients when Garron was away. They have accomplished a great deal in their work, and have been through so much. They have grown close, and for that reason, Nelson feels like a son to Garron.

Today, the FOTCOH surgery team has performed close to 1,200 surgeries with no deaths and no major complications. Garron Lukas is the only surgeon who has ever worked with FOTCOH.

*

The FOTCOH Child Sponsorship Program was born accidentally. It started when Dick met a young Haitian girl named Natasha.

When Dick first met her, Natasha was eight years old. Before the clinic was built, when the medical team was still working at the Sea of Love, a group of Haitian children were playing

CHAPTER 10: DIS

soccer one evening to entertain the volunteers. Dick noticed that one little girl in particular was a fantastic soccer player. She was fast, and had total control of the ball. But as Dick watched her, enthralled by her talent, he noticed that she wasn't moving quite right—she had a brace on her foot, which made it difficult for her to walk, let alone run.

Natasha had a clubfoot. A birth defect, a clubfoot causes the bones in the feet to turn inwards. Because of this deformity, a person will either walk on their ankles or the sides of their feet. Dick was so impressed by Natasha's skills, despite the challenge her foot created, that he wanted to do something to correct her clubfoot. He spoke with her parents, and they agreed to let Dick help. Within a few weeks, he found an organization in Port-au-Prince that could perform the surgery, and he scheduled an appointment.

Natasha responded well to the surgery. Shortly after the procedure and some physical therapy, she was able to walk without difficulty, and she no longer needed a brace on her foot. Other than a few scars, no one would have guessed she ever had a problem. After Natasha returned to Jacmel, Dick figured he couldn't see having her foot corrected and then not making sure she went to school. In Haiti, no child gets an education for free. It costs money to attend school, and uniforms and school supplies are an additional expense. Many families do not send their children to school because they can't afford the tuition.

Dick and Barb decided to sponsor Natasha, making sure she had money for school fees. Over the next few years, they started sponsoring a few other children that they met along the way. Once the clinic construction was complete, the interest in sponsorship really began to grow. The medical volunteers wanted to know how they could help the young patients they were treating, knowing their families had no money for school for their children.

Since Barb was now retired and in Haiti most of the year, she decided to make the sponsorship program official. She started by writing down information about the children who visited the clinic—she recorded their names, their birthdays, and the towns they lived in. She then took photos of the children and created a packet to give out to FOTCOH supporters back home. The response was huge. Hundreds of people agreed to sponsor children, and before she knew it, Barb had her hands full.

After the sponsorship program took off, Barb got some of the non-medical volunteers involved in keeping the children in the program organized. She even created a special Sponsorship Week for the volunteers to come to Haiti, separate from the medical team, just to work on updating child profiles and take new pictures for the sponsors back home. When the volunteers were not in Haiti, Boyer made sure the families received the funds and that the children's reports cards were periodically turned in so sponsors knew the children were attending school.

At its peak, nearly 380 Haitian children were enrolled in the program, most of whom Barb could name just by seeing them at the clinic.

*

Dick met Gerald when he was around ten years old, back when the clinic was still under construction. Thin and small for his age, Gerald carried tools for Boss Ken. He followed Boss Ken around, lugging hammers and buckets of nails. Gerald did whatever Boss Ken asked of him, and he worked hard, trying to learn the trade. He was a smart and sweet kid—Dick never saw him look unhappy on the job site.

CHAPTER 10: DIS

Dick saw Gerald working with Boss Ken almost every day, and he would chat with him here and there. One morning, Gerald showed Dick some drawings he had made of construction plans, and Dick was blown away—here was such a young boy with all these big ideas. He asked Gerald why he wasn't in school. He said he didn't go to school because he had to work. Dick asked him if he was getting paid to help Boss Ken, and Gerald said no—he was an apprentice.

Dick stopped the conversation and went to look for Boss Ken. When he found him, he asked him why Gerald wasn't in school. Boss Ken said the boy wanted to learn, so he was teaching him. Dick was not satisfied with the answer—he felt Gerald needed to get an education. Boss Ken argued that Gerald did not make enough money to pay for school. Dick shot back, stating he understood that Gerald didn't make any money at all.

Dick insisted that starting the next day, Gerald was going to school. He could work with Boss Ken in the morning, or after school, but he was going to go to school every day. From then on, Gerald went to school, and Dick and Barb made sure he had money to attend. As he got older, Gerald had many other sponsors who supported him through the sponsorship program. After finishing primary and secondary school, Gerald went on to a university in Port-au-Prince to study civil engineering.

*

When Dick met Milo, he looked like a fish, his skin resembling white scales as the result of an unknown skin disease. No doctor in Jacmel could determine the cause, so Milo had never been treated. He was a small boy, only about eight years old, and his condition caused his skin to be constantly irritated. Because of the way it made Milo look, it also made him an outcast.

Milo was in absolute misery. He wanted to die.

Milo's father brought him to the clinic to see if the medical team could do anything for his son. The doctors determined that Milo's case was so rare that they would not be able to care for him. Wanting desperately to help Milo, Dick made arrangements for him to see a specialist. He found an American dermatologist in Port-au-Prince that would see Milo as soon as he and his father could get there. Dick sent them to the city, with money for transportation, food, and lodging. Thankfully, the doctor was able to find the cause of Milo's skin problem. He was prescribed special ointments and instructed on how to care for his skin.

When Milo came back to Jacmel with his father, Barb enrolled him in the sponsorship program. Again, Dick and Barb didn't want to just get Milo treated without making sure he could go to school. And, thanks to many sponsors over the years, Milo went through primary school, secondary school, and then on to medical school in the Dominican Republic.

Though the FOTCOH Child Sponsorship Program grew quite large, after more than fifteen years of sponsoring children in Haiti, the program was canceled. As Barb started to get older, it had become much harder for her to handle all the responsibility, and no other volunteers were in Haiti often enough to take over for her. Although Boyer had always been very helpful, the program was taking away from his responsibilities managing the clinic, and, though it was hard to do, it simply became time to end it. Even though the program ended, Dick and Barb were grateful for what they had been able to do with the help of many sponsors for such a long time. And more so, they were incredibly proud of all the Haitian children they had the privilege of watching grow up.

CHAPTER 10: DIS

*

Dick and Barb had been through many storms and hurricanes in Haiti. At times, fallen trees and scattered debris had caused considerable damage to the clinic property. But nothing compared to the 2010 earthquake, not only in its destruction, but in the response it received in regards to emergency relief. The earthquake left some parts of Haiti in complete shambles as hundreds of thousands of buildings collapsed. Because so many buildings were not adequately reinforced, seemingly sturdy concrete structures toppled within seconds during the earthquake, or shortly after.

In Port-au-Prince, the most populated city in Haiti, the earthquake's impact caused monumental damage and devastation. The Presidential Palace and the Port-au-Prince Cathedral collapsed. Government buildings crumbled to the ground, killing a quarter of the country's civil servants. Hospitals and health care facilities fell. Hotels, schools, churches, jails, and houses went down in a matter of seconds. In and around the capital, roads were destroyed, and phone service went out, making it difficult for rescue workers to communicate with one another, as well as locate the injured, or those that were trapped under rubble.

Estimates put the number of dead in Haiti following the earthquake between 220,000 and 315,000. The number of injured is thought to be just as high. One and a half million people were displaced. Thirteen hundred camps were set up in the country, as 600,000 people left the capital to find refuge. Over 100,000 homes were completely destroyed, and nearly 200,000 were badly damaged. Nearly 19 million cubic meters of rubble filled the streets of Port-au-Prince after the earthquake. Those that lost their homes slept on the street, in parks or in cars, or were moved to tent camps set up by the government. Many of the displaced lived in camps for years after the earthquake, with little protection from weather or crime, and without proper sanitation and little access to clean water. The earthquake is estimated to have caused over $14 billion in destruction. In all, nearly 3.5 million people living in Haiti were affected, or one-third of the population.

*

It took two days and eight separate flights to get the entire medical team to the clinic after the earthquake. The team arrived one or two at a time. Garron was already scheduled to fly to Haiti that January. After his flight was rerouted, he ended up being one of the first volunteers to arrive to Jacmel. While they waited for the rest of the team to arrive, Dick and Boyer took Garron around town to see the scope of the destruction.

By the time Garron had landed in Haiti, over a week had passed since the earthquake hit. Aid organizations had already swarmed into Jacmel. The amount of aid was enormous, not only in terms of the number of relief workers, but in terms of supplies—food, water in plastic bottles and bags, tents, medications, and medical supplies flooded the town in an unorganized manner. Garron was taken aback by the chaos—as they walked through the center of Jacmel, where the aid organizations were stationed, there didn't seem to be any coordination among groups. It was difficult to tell what teams had which supplies, and who was distributing them. It didn't seem as though anyone really knew what was happening.

Garron was also seeing a number of people in town with injuries caused by the earthquake. He mainly saw crushed hands, arms, and legs from those who had been inside buildings that collapsed. He came to refer to the situation in the days right after the earthquake as "Civil War medicine"— people with crushed limbs who had lost hope in saving them began using hardware store saws to perform desperate amputations.

Within a few days of arriving, Garron began taking patients at the clinic to schedule surgeries for the upcoming weeks. As he would find out soon enough, performing surgery in the aftermath of the earthquake would be trying. One of the main issues was the aftershocks. Within nine hours of the earthquake, thirty-two aftershocks were recorded. And although the number decreased in the days following the earthquake, they continued for weeks.

Haitians were terrified of the aftershocks, which wasn't surprising to Garron. So many of them had lost their homes, just like Nelson had, in the earthquake. Others had not only lost their house, but had watched their families perish within it. The surgery team was deeply frightened every time the hospital shook. Not only was Garron continuously interrupted during surgery because of the aftershocks themselves, but he also had to contend with everyone running out of the building whenever one occurred. Garron would then have to go outside and try to talk everyone into coming back inside so he could finish the surgery.

But Garron knew he was fortunate to be able to perform surgeries at all—without the FOTCOH surgery program, he would not have had proper equipment and surgical supplies, let alone a place to perform surgery. And because of that, he was able to do more than other surgeons who had come to Haiti after the earthquake without similar resources. One of the Haitian patients Garron was able to help was a young girl, around eight or nine years old, who had lost her entire family when their house collapsed. She survived, but with a badly crushed hand. Garron operated on the girl's hand four times in two weeks, and he was able to not only save it, but preserve some mobility, although limited.

It had been such a sad time in Haiti for everyone, including Garron. He was happy he had been able to do something nice to help the little girl. He proudly displays a picture of her in his office at home.

*

As Garron performed surgeries at the hospital, the rest of the medical team remained at the clinic, busily seeing patients. On top of treating patients with injuries from the earthquake, the volunteers were still seeing their regularly scheduled patients, making their workload much larger than normal.

Dick remembered the clinic running smoothly in the weeks after the quake, even within the heightened urgency of the situation. One such emergency involved a set of newborn twins who were brought to the clinic. Because their mother had high blood pressure, the twins had been born extremely premature, and they struggled to survive. When the tiny babies arrived, the entire medical team worked together to try to save their lives. They improvised incubators out of Mylar and window frames and mixed up preemie formula for them. They took turns staying up all night to monitor the twins. Since the babies were too premature to feed with a bottle, they had to be fed using feeding tubes.

The next morning, the team knew they could no longer care for the twins—the clinic did not have the supplies or the personnel to continue the rigorous schedule of watching over them, and the team had hundreds of other patients waiting for

CHAPTER 10: DIS

treatment. The babies had also started to show signs of apnea, meaning they would require more sophisticated monitoring. The team urgently needed to get the twins to Port-au-Prince where other aid organizations would be more equipped to care for them. Fortunately, a medical volunteer on the team worked in emergency response at a hospital in the United States, and because of his connections, he was able to reach a Canadian team that agreed to take the twins to Port-au-Prince in an army helicopter. He and another team member traveled with the babies to the Toussaint Louverture International Airport where they delivered them to a great medical team from Israel, relieved knowing they were in good hands.

*

The team left Haiti after two weeks. Although they had done a lot of good work helping patients recover from injuries from the earthquake, it would be many years before Haiti itself would begin to recover. Clean up and construction in the country was slow. It often seemed as if Jacmel was being rebuilt one brick at a time. Sometimes it didn't feel like any progress was being made. Dick never did see construction equipment in town removing the rubble, causing him, and many other people, to wonder where the aid money went and what was really being done to help Haiti rebuild.

After the earthquake, $13.5 billion was donated or pledged for relief efforts. But, despite the influx of money to support and rebuild in Haiti, less than half of one percent of the funds went to Haitian NGOs. Only one percent of funds went to the Haitian government. More than ninety percent of funding went to either international NGOs, private contractors, UN agencies, or never left the country in which it was donated. Relief aid mostly went to providing food, water, tarps, and tents in the months and years after the earthquake, which, while necessary for the short term, did not create lasting change for the Haitian people.

Dick felt like money was being wasted in the aftermath of the earthquake. It still bothers him to this day. To him it seemed like money was being spent frivolously. He saw relief workers driving around in huge, brand new vehicles, paying exorbitant rent for places to stay in Jacmel. He never saw Haitians hired to do any real work. They were hired to do simple jobs like sweeping up trash in the street or working as drivers. Sometimes they worked as interpreters. But Haitians were not hired to rebuild in their own country. The NGOs hired employees and contractors coming from the United States, France, and Canada, to name a few, and that money went back to those countries—it didn't stay in Haiti. It just didn't seem like the money was being spent on the Haitian people. It didn't make sense to Dick. He didn't see why Haitians weren't hired to do the work, to build their own buildings.

And Dick wasn't the only one who felt that way. When the NGOs started arriving in Jacmel after the earthquake, Boyer had been offered jobs, but he turned them all down. He knew they wouldn't stay in Haiti long, and he didn't want short-lived employment. And he was right. A few years after the earthquake, the NGOs started disappearing. Having only had a plan to work for a certain number of years in Haiti—maybe one, or two, or three—the larger NGOs left when that time was up, sometimes whether their projects were completed or not.

Boyer wanted something more sustainable in his life—something he could rely on. And even though those NGOs could have paid him more, he knew it wasn't going to last, and he knew the work wouldn't be as rewarding. Working for Dick was

CHAPTER 10: DIS

different. Dick owned land, and he hired Haitians, and the clinic was permanent. Dick believed that money spent should stay in Haiti as much as possible. That is what mattered to Boyer, and he knew that is what mattered to Haiti and its people. He knew he could trust that Dick and the medical teams would be there for the Haitians. They had been coming to Haiti long before the earthquake, and he knew he could depend on them being in Haiti long after.

*

For years after the earthquake, Dick would remember a man by the name of Gensel Augustine. Augustine had found a little boy, only a toddler, underneath the rubble of a fallen building in Jacmel, mostly unharmed. Augustine pulled the boy out from the debris and took him home. Soon after, he brought the boy to the clinic to see if he could get some food and clothing for the child, as well as have him examined by a doctor.

After telling the team the story of how he found the boy, Augustine explained he had not wished to keep him if his family was looking for him. He had tried to find his family—he even took the boy to the police station so they could announce the child's description over the radio. But after a few weeks, no one had claimed him. The police determined the family must have vanished in the earthquake. Augustine already knew he wanted to take care of him, even before hearing this news, and he gladly adopted the boy as his son, a first child for Augustine and his wife. And because of how he came into Augustine's life, he named the boy Godson.

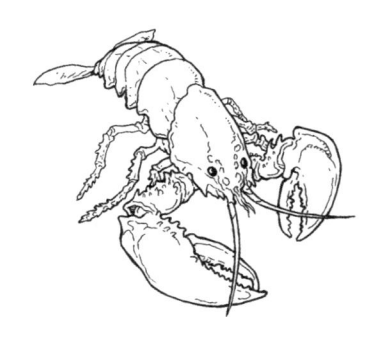

onz

Geographically, Haiti is very diverse. Here at the clinic the view from the upper balcony is paradise. We are surrounded by beautiful tropical foliage, turquoise water and green mountains. If we walk or drive just a little way down the road we see tiny houses or tent like structures housing an entire family. We see muddy roads and garbage lined streets. We see unimaginable poverty.

The Haitian patients we see are just as diverse. We have seen sick and starving infants that we try to help by providing nutrition for them and education for their mothers so that the babies can become healthy and thrive. We try to offer them hope and pray that we will see them come back to us for well baby checks. We also see babies that are healthy and happy as a result of this care. We see elderly patients that we treat for hypertension and diabetes. Some of these patients have lived far beyond the expected life span here in Haiti. We see sick patients who require other care such as surgery, wound care, breathing treatments and much more. They come to the clinic—the sick, the young, and the old, from near and far to seek what we have to offer them: medical care, education and most of all, hope.

It takes a lot to put these mission trips together. Preparation begins long before the team arrives in Haiti. Each trip requires donations from generous supporters, team leaders who dedicate time and energy to plan and facilitate each mission, individuals who order supplies and medications, volunteers who dedicate their time and money to come to Haiti. The team members come from different places and walks of life all for the same purpose.

Once a year, for the past three years, I have been blessed, honored, and humbled to travel to Haiti to work with a team to provide care to the grateful and gracious Haitian people.

-Paula, Non-Medical Volunteer
May 2015

CHAPTER 11: ONZ

When Dick fell and hit his head, he was alone with Barb in the clinic. It was the summer of 2010, and they had both turned seventy-three years old. In the years to come, Dick and Barb would begin to understand how much tougher it would be to run the clinic when their health, and security, were at risk—like so many Haitians felt every day of their lives. Despite the new challenges ahead and the adversity they would face, they were not going to give up, no matter how much harder it would become to live and work in Haiti. When others might have walked away, Dick and Barb were determined to keep going back.

Dick was upstairs on his computer when he heard the phone ringing in the kitchen. When Barb didn't answer, he got up from his chair and walked over to the railing of the staircase to look for her. When he leaned over, he passed out. He fell down the stairs, landing on the platform between the second and third floor.

Barb didn't actually see Dick fall—the first sign that something was wrong was a moaning sound coming from the stairs. She had been standing in the kitchen, washing dishes and hadn't heard the phone. When she shut off the sink and turned around to check for the source of the sound, she saw Dick lying limply on the platform. She ran up to him and rolled him over to check if he was breathing. He was, but he had lost consciousness.

Barb needed to get help right away. She knew she couldn't move Dick herself. She ran down the stairs to the first floor and out of the clinic. As fast as she could move, she made her way towards a small house about one hundred meters from the clinic where Esperidon, the groundskeeper, lived with his family, just inside the clinic gate.

"Esperidon! Dick tonbe! Dick tonbe! Dick fell down!" Barb yelled in a panic as she reached the house.

Louinel, Esperidon's son, heard Barb's cry and shot out of the door of the house, running at full speed toward the clinic, followed rapidly by Esperidon. Barb turned and tried her hardest to keep up with them.

When they reached Dick, he was awake, but going in and out of consciousness. They got him up off the floor and carried him to bed. Louinel called Boyer. When he didn't pick up the phone, Louinel began to panic. He left the clinic to search for Boyer himself.

Esperidon kept an eye on Dick, while Barb called Nelson. He answered and told Barb he would be at the clinic as soon as he could. When Nelson arrived twenty minutes later, Dick was awake and able to sit up in bed. Nelson could tell he was tired as he was talking, and he wasn't communicating fluidly. Nelson was worried. Because of Dick's age, falling down could mean a serious problem. Nelson called Garron in the United States and asked for his advice. Garron instructed Nelson to get Dick evacuated to Ft. Lauderdale immediately. He knew that no advanced diagnostic imaging facilities were available in Haiti, and neurosurgery capabilities were limited. Considering the type of head injury Dick had sustained, a subdural or epidural hematoma was a real possibility and would require urgent attention. Nelson hung up the phone and told Dick and Barb what Garron had said—Dick required a CAT scan and needed to leave Haiti as soon as possible.

Barb and Dick had evacuation insurance for situations like this, but they had never had to use it before. Barb ran to get the contact information for Medjet Assist from Dick's desk. When she came back with the number, Nelson made the call. He explained to the Medjet representative that it was imperative that Dick be flown out of the country, because it was not possible for

CHAPTER 11: ONZ

him to get a CAT scan in Haiti, not even in Port-au-Prince. It had only been about six months since the earthquake, and Haiti was still a mess—in many places, it still looked like the earthquake had just happened.

After some convincing of Nelson's medical expertise, the Medjet representative agreed to have Dick evacuated, but a plane couldn't pick him up in Jacmel—the runway at the airport was too short. Dick was going to have to get to Port-au-Prince first. Barb thought for a moment and decided to contact Missionary Aviation Fellowship, or MAF. MAF serves people in remote areas, sometimes in emergency situations. They mainly work in impoverished countries. When not providing flights to assist with aid relief, MAF was available for private chartered flights. Dick and Barb frequently hired them to fly the medical teams between Port-au-Prince and Jacmel.

Barb called the MAF office, and a young woman answered. After a confusing conversation about whether Barb had a reservation, Dick chimed in and told Barb to ask for Will. Will was one of MAF's pilots. They had flown with Will many times, and Dick was comfortable asking for him by name, especially in a situation like this. Will got on the phone a few minutes later, and Barb explained what was happening. Will told her he would call her back in two minutes, and hung up the phone. By the time he returned Barb's call a few minutes later, he had already made the arrangements—a plane would be at the Jacmel airport within hours.

Almost as soon as Barb hung up the phone, Boyer came running up the stairs of the clinic to the bedroom. While Boyer and Nelson helped Dick out of bed, Barb hurried to pack their bags. Barb, Dick, Nelson and Boyer drove to the Jacmel airport, where Dick and Barb said nervous goodbyes and boarded the

MAF plane. Once they got to Port-au-Prince, a few hours went by before the Medjet Assist plane was ready to take them to Florida.

By the time Dick and Barb landed in Ft. Lauderdale that evening, and Dick was taken to the hospital, fourteen hours had passed since he had hit his head. Barb thought that was about as speedy as it would be. If Dick had had a heart attack in Haiti, they would have never gotten him somewhere in time. But even then, if it had not been for Nelson's efforts in talking to Garron and Medjet Assist, they might not have gotten Dick out that day at all.

Dick's doctor did find bleeding in his brain—a hematoma, just as Garron had thought. He had most likely passed out due to low blood pressure. He was in the hospital for a week and afterward was sent home to rest. His doctors asked him to take it easy for a few months while he was monitored and observed, which he tried to do the best he could, all the while wishing he could get back to Haiti and the clinic. He knew that everything would be fine without him. The volunteers and Haitian staff would make sure that everything was running as usual, but he still wanted to return as soon as he could. Nothing could keep him away, not even concerns for his health. It was a force that pulled him in.

Dick and Barb missed two clinics as Dick recovered at home.

*

When Barb fell down at the clinic, in early 2011, her situation was much less of an emergency than Dick's had been—at least, at first. After returning from dinner at the Hotel Cyvadier one evening, Barb went into the bedroom and Dick went to the bathroom. Suddenly, Dick heard a *splat* sound.

CHAPTER 11: ONZ

"Barb? Barb!" he yelled.

Barb did not respond. Dick left the bathroom to look for her. He found her sprawled out on her back next to the dresser, looking straight up at the ceiling. She was conscious, but she looked stunned. She had no idea how she ended up on the floor.

Dick helped Barb up, and she went straight to bed. The following day, she felt a slight pain in her leg. Over the next few weeks, the pain got worse and worse, and eventually she was barely able to walk across the kitchen. She started using a cane so she could move around comfortably.

After returning to Ft. Lauderdale a few months later, Barb had her leg checked out. She had an MRI, but her doctor could not find anything out of the ordinary. They told her the pain was most likely a result of arthritis and suggested she continue to walk with the assistance of the cane.

In June of the same year, Dick and Barb went to Peoria to visit family and friends and to attend a FOTCOH board meeting. They were staying at their grandson's house while in town. As they were leaving to go to the meeting, Barb fell down in the driveway. She tried to get up on her own, but she couldn't move. Dick rushed her to the hospital. This time, it was clear that she had a broken leg, although they had thought all along that it was possible she had a small fracture or break from her previous fall in the clinic, nearly six months before.

Barb had a rod inserted into her leg and had to stay in the hospital for a few weeks before she could go home. She did not want to be in the hospital. It was terrible for her to be immobile and not able to do things for herself. She was miserable, and it made it worse knowing that she wouldn't be able to go back to Haiti with Dick for a while. Because of her broken leg, she missed the July and September clinics while she recovered. It was the first time she and Dick had not been to Haiti together in ten years, since Barb had retired.

Although the team stepped up to take on her responsibilities, it was tough not having Barb at the clinic. Because she had always handled all the shopping, the volunteers didn't know what was available at the markets. And no one knew how to do inventory for the kitchen, so when it came time to take stock of the food before leaving, the team wasn't sure how to make a grocery list for the next team to replenish supplies. Barb had always been in charge of cooking, and she was the only one who knew which items were harder to find in Haiti, like refried beans, cheese, and pancake mix. Or items like peanut butter, lemonade mix, paper towels, and toilet paper that were much cheaper to purchase in the United States. She wasn't there to organize the records either, which slowed down the team a bit, because Barb was just so fast at getting the records in order. It just wasn't the same for the team, or Dick, without Barb at the clinic.

*

Dick and Barb weren't dealing only with health issues in Haiti in the years immediately following the earthquake. They were also dealing with security issues, and it wasn't just them that was worried—the whole town of Jacmel was concerned. In early 2012, a gang robbed a local orphanage and a hotel in town. To make matters worse, the police thought the thieves had inside information that was allowing them to pull off the robberies without getting caught. The thieves were targeting people who were taking large sums of money out of the bank. Every two or three months, someone who had just made a large withdrawal would get robbed. It became apparent that these people were being targeted before they had a chance to spend or distribute

CHAPTER 11: ONZ

the cash.

The authorities had not been able to catch any of the gang members for over a year. The police grew suspicious that some of their own officers were the ones tipping off the thieves, so new policemen had been brought into Jacmel and some of the existing officers had been transferred to other areas. Still the robberies continued.

Dick and Barb were concerned about the safety of the clinic and the volunteers. They were also worried about the Haitian staff—it made them uneasy to think that someone might be watching Boyer when he went to the bank. They decided it was time to hire a full-time security guard. Boyer recommended a local man named Williams Toussaint, a large, quiet Haitian known for his kindness, but also his capacity to intimidate. As soon as he was hired, Williams began patrolling the clinic every night.

One night not long after Williams began working for Dick and Barb, the couple was asleep in their room when they awoke to the sound of a shotgun. They were alone in the clinic. Dick jumped out of bed, grabbed his pistol out of the dresser drawer, and looked out the window. He shouted to Barb to stay down away from the windows, behind the bed.

"Williams! Are you out there?" Dick yelled.

No one yelled back.

Dick left the bedroom and went out onto the balcony. He could see Williams lying quietly on top of the generator depot, roughly forty feet away from the clinic, gun raised. By the way Williams had his gun aimed, Dick could tell he had his eye on someone in the distance. Dick walked around to the other side of the balcony, attempting to remain quiet, all the while trying to see for himself if someone was down below. Williams sent out a shot to scare off whomever was on the property, and continued to shoot. He sent out eight or nine shots in about two minutes. To Dick and Barb, it felt like it went on forever. When he was sure that it was safe, Williams called Dick from his cell phone to let him know whoever was there had climbed over the wall and was gone.

The next day, Dick and Barb told Boyer about what had happened. They had been planning to go home a few days later, but after the incident, Boyer insisted that they leave Haiti much sooner. He had some inside information—people in Jacmel still believed that corruption in the police force was the reason for the robberies, despite the previous change in officers. The people of Jacmel were fed up. In protest, they were going to set up roadblocks all over town. Such road blocks, made by stacking rocks, tree limbs, and old tires into large piles to prevent vehicles from passing, are a common means for protest in Haiti. To make sure roadblocks aren't taken down, Haitians will stand guard in the street, protecting the newly formed barriers or, sometimes, even set fire to the roadblocks. Boyer wanted Dick and Barb to leave Jacmel before things got out of control—before they couldn't get out.

That afternoon, Dick and Barb packed up the truck and headed towards Port-au-Prince, accompanied by Boyer. They went through four roadblocks on their way out of town. Each time, they were only allowed to pass if either Boyer knew the people manning the roadblocks, or the Haitians knew Dick and Barb from the clinic. Once, they had to pay their way through.

Fortunately, although creating a great deal of chaos, the roadblocks worked for the people of Jacmel. The police force changed once again, and the robbers were caught not long after. The robberies stopped all together. There has not been another

CHAPTER 11: ONZ

incident at the clinic since.

*

 Dick and Barb returned to Haiti a few months later, in the summer of 2012. Toward the end of the year, they went home to Ft. Lauderdale to get ready for a trip to Washington state to visit family for Christmas. A few days before leaving, Dick went to his cardiologist for a scheduled endoscopy.
 When Dick's cardiologist examined him, he found that Dick's pulse rate was in the low thirties, causing much alarm. The doctor believed Dick's arteries were blocked. He canceled the endoscopy and instead ordered an angiogram. If the angiogram showed blockage, Dick would stay in the hospital to have surgery the next day.
 Dick's doctor was correct—he did need surgery, and right away. Their vacation plans were canceled—he would not be leaving the hospital. With little time to think about what was happening, Barb got busy calling family and friends, including some of the volunteers they were close to. She knew quite a few of them would be worried about Dick. Barb especially wanted to make sure she talked to Garron. They considered him to be a good friend, and since he was a surgeon, Barb knew he could shed some light on what Dick could expect from his surgery. After Barb got off the phone with him, Garron called Dick to talk to him directly.
 Garron was forward with Dick. He told him that after the surgery, he was going to hurt like hell—he would be in pain like he had never been before. He told him the only way he was going to survive was to make up his mind ahead of time to survive. In the end, he would feel better, even though it would be a long recovery. Dick appreciated Garron's call, and, although he was

nervous, he felt better having heard from someone he trusted, who could offer him such important advice, which he took very seriously. Just as Garron had said, Dick made up his mind to survive.

Dick's surgery was scheduled for December 12, 2012. He was seventy-four years old. As he was being prepped for the procedure, he talked to his nurse, a Haitian man. Their conversation took Dick's mind off the surgery for a little while, and he enjoyed chatting with someone who he could relate to so well. Dick asked his nurse where he was from in Haiti and told him about the clinic. By the time he was ready for surgery, Dick was less anxious. He thought it felt like a sign—having a Haitian nurse meant he was in good hands.

Dick had an aortic valve replacement, a mitral valve repair, quadruple bypass surgery, and he received a pacemaker. The surgery went well, but the healing process was arduous, just as Garron said it would be. Dick never could have imagined how long he would feel the effects of his surgery. Today, he still doesn't feel great all the time. He wishes he felt better. His body gets more tired, and it creaks more. His feet hurt, and his back. He feels that the surgery slowed him down. But he made it through the surgery, and for that he is incredibly grateful. He knows he wouldn't have been around much longer if he hadn't gone through with it.

Because of Dick's surgery, he and Barb missed their trip to Washington, as well as the January clinic. Barb went back to Haiti in February and stayed through March. It was the first time that Barb had ever been to Haiti without Dick.

Dick would talk to Barb on the phone while she was in Haiti without him and try to offer his help, but he could tell he wasn't being told everything that was going on at the clinic. He knew

CHAPTER 11: ONZ

Barb didn't want to cause him stress during his recovery. But she sounded tired every time they spoke, and Dick worried that it was too much for her to do on her own. She had a lot on her plate. Even with the help of Boyer, her added workload was immense—making sure the interpreters were available to work, making arrangements for transporting patients to other facilities when necessary, making plans for children from the local schools to be seen at the clinic, scheduling repairs, writing receipts, doing payroll. The list went on and on.

And Dick was right. Barb was exhausted. She was worn out, and she wasn't sleeping. The team was doing just fine, but Barb had taken on too much. She was still cooking and filing dossiers, but now she was also managing the staff, and scheduling outings for the team. The tiles of the kitchen had started to come up off the concrete and break apart, creating mounds on the floor, causing her even more stress. Although she knew it was from natural wear and tear on the building, she was overwhelmed without Dick there.

By the time Barb got back to Ft. Lauderdale, Dick practically had to scrape her up off the curb at the airport. When he pulled up to the arrival lane to pick her up, Barb plopped down in the passenger seat and closed the door, so tired she looked like she was about to cry. Dick looked at her, and then looked out the passenger-side window. Barb, completely drained, had gotten in the car, not even realizing she had left all her bags on the curb.

*

After Dick's surgery, both Dick and Barb's doctors weren't excited about them continuing to travel to Haiti. They wanted them to slow down, and recommended that they stop going to the clinic altogether. It was not something they insisted on, but they said it would be better for the pair's health. The doctors made their point, and Dick and Barb politely made theirs as well. They promised to cut down on traveling, but they would not stop going to Haiti. Neither of them wanted to be done. As they were getting older, it was becoming harder for them, but they were more determined than ever to continue their work. The Haitians and the volunteers still depended on them, and they just couldn't stay away. It just wasn't time.

Dick returned to the clinic with Barb in May 2012, less than six months after his open-heart surgery.

douz

Hi, my name is Richard Hammond. My wife, Barbara, and I founded Friends of the Children of Haiti. With the help of many Haitians, we built a clinic in Haiti for our medical program and living quarters for our volunteers.

During the years since the completion of the building, I have missed four clinics. Barb has missed five. I missed both the January and March clinics recently because I had open-heart surgery in December.

I was very apprehensive about returning for the May clinic, being concerned about the condition of the building since my absence, and repairs that might be needed because of normal wear and tear, as well as damages that occurred during the earthquake a few years ago. We were here when the earthquake hit and we have survived several hurricanes. I was also concerned about how I was going to be physically. I was still weak from my surgery.

When I arrived my concerns were forgotten. Repairs still needed to be done, but my feeling of anxiety was replaced only with feelings of happiness. The Haitians greeted me with an overwhelming reception. Everyone I saw said they were happy to see me.

"Kouman ou ye, Papa? Nou ap kontan ke ou te retounen li ban nou".
How are you, Papa? We are happy that you have returned to us."

We prayed together and we laughed together.

When the medical team arrived we were greeted with the normal concerns of the new volunteers and excitement from the veterans who were returning to the clinic. The first day was spent unpacking, organizing, preparing for the clinic, having dinner, and finally sleeping.

The next morning clinic began with a bang. The volunteers met the Haitian interpreters and other workers, and everyone went to work. Everything went well. There was no first day apprehension. If there was, it was forgotten rapidly.

The clinic functioned great. Garron, our surgeon, scheduled surgeries for the duration of the clinic. Beth, the team leader, kept the Haitian patients moving at a good pace. Steve, the oral surgeon, did the same. The entire clinic worked very well.

I was at peace.

Someday the Lord is going to call Barb and I home. I promise you this. The clinic will still be functioning, maybe even better than now, although I don't know what that will be like. We will be watching

CHAPTER 12: DOUZ

and giving our support.

I am proud that the Lord chose Barb and I to organize FOTCOH. I am proud of all that has been accomplished over the years.

I am proud of the people who have given up their time with their families. I am proud of the families who have given up their mothers, their fathers, sisters, and brothers so they can help people so far away from home.

I am proud of the relationship that has developed between the Haitians and our teams. The Haitians have learned a lot about health care from us. We have learned a lot about life.

-Dick, Cofounder, Friends of the Children of Haiti
May 2013

One afternoon in early 2005, Dick was driving through Jacmel on his way to pick up Garron from the Dr. Martinez Hospital. Garron had finished up his last day of surgery, which meant that in just a few short days, the team would be flying home, having wrapped up another two weeks of clinic.

As he was making his way through town, Dick heard someone yell his name on the street. He stopped the truck and looked around. He didn't see anyone at first. Again, a voice yelled, "Dick!" This time, he turned to see a young woman running toward the car. Dick knew her. She was one of Father LaBourne's adopted children, Marie Claude, all grown up. Dick had known her for more than thirty years by then, for as long as he had been coming to Haiti.

She approached the window, saying "Bonswa," and then asked Dick to wait there for a moment. She had something for him in her house. She hurried away and a few minutes later reappeared with a large, flat package wrapped in brown paper.

"What is this?" Dick asked.

She started to unwrap the package, carefully pulling away the paper piece by piece, until Dick could see that it was a canvas painting mounted on a wooden frame. The painting was a portrait of him.

Marie Claude handed the painting to Dick through the window of the truck.

"From the people, for what you do for Haiti," she said. "To thank you."

Dick was stunned.

Dick thanked her for the gift and said goodbye, continuing on to the hospital. After he picked up Garron, they returned to the clinic. The team was done working for the day and had gone to the beach. The clinic was empty, except for Barb. Dick parked

CHAPTER 12: DOUZ

the truck and took the painting out. As he walked toward the clinic, he realized he was embarrassed about having a portrait of himself. He appreciated that it had been a gift from the community, but he wasn't sure if he was ready for anyone to see it, not even Barb. Before he went in, he wrapped the painting back in its paper. Once inside, he snuck the painting up the stairs and put it in the bedroom closet, then went to the kitchen to help Barb with dinner.

That evening, when the team returned, everyone gathered in the kitchen to eat. The atmosphere during the meal was light and festive. The team loudly chatted about their day, the patients they had seen, and the funny stories their Haitian interpreters had told them. As Dick sat at one of the plastic tables with a few of the volunteers, he thought about how wonderful it was to be surrounded by such loving people, some dear friends, some longtime volunteers, and some who had been strangers to him only two weeks before. He was grateful for everyone in the room. As he looked around, he reminded himself that everyone was there for the same reason, whether for the first time or the tenth: because they all believed in the work that was being done at the clinic—because they believed in what Dick and Barb had started in Haiti. Because they believed in the Haitian people.

Dick was no longer embarrassed about the painting. Instead, he felt proud of the people who were thoughtful enough to give him such a remarkable present. He decided he wanted to show off his gift.

Dick stood up from his chair and announced to the team that he had something he wanted them to see. The volunteers sat silently, having stopped their lively conversations, as they watched Dick slowly walk up the stairs. When he came back down to the kitchen, he had the painting in his hands. As he began to unwrap it, he found that he was even more in awe of it than he had been when he saw it earlier in the day. The portrait was incredibly realistic. It was a bust of Dick wearing a white shirt. His head was slightly tilted, and he was smiling, his eyes facing forward. It wasn't a large painting, but the details of his face were impressive. He turned the painting around to show the team, and Barb. They were astounded. It was a beautiful portrait—a true testament to the love the Haitian people had for Dick, and for the clinic.

After receiving such a tremendous reaction from the volunteers, Dick knew he wanted to display the painting. But one thing was missing. He wanted a portrait of Barb to go right beside his, because she deserved to have one too. If Barb had never gotten in touch with Harry so many years before, Dick never would have gone back to Haiti. And without all of Barb's efforts in fundraising, the clinic would not be there either. Without each other, neither of them would have been able to accomplish what they did.

Dick asked Boyer to find out who the artist was that painted the portrait. It turned out to be a local painter who had a studio in Jacmel. They went to visit him. Dick asked the artist about the painting, and what he would need to paint one exactly the same way, but of Barb. The man said he had painted Dick's portrait by looking at a photo. The next day, Dick returned to the studio with a picture of Barb.

Once Barb's painting was finished, Dick hung them both side by side in the clinic. Now, he had the total gift.

*

In February 2014, I visited Dick and Barb in Haiti. It was the first time I had been to the clinic without a medical team.

CHAPTER 12: DOUZ

I flew to Port-au-Prince alone, and Boyer picked me up from the airport. We made the drive to Jacmel, stopping a few times so he could take care of some business—picking up a freezer, purchasing minutes for his cell phone, buying chicken and rice from a food stand on the side of the road.

We arrived at the clinic late, close to midnight. But despite the hour, Dick and Barb had waited up for us, like parents wait for their children to come home. Boyer left shortly after, and I stayed up chatting with Dick and Barb, helping myself to a Prestige out of the fridge.

We talked about how Dick got started working in Haiti so many years before, and all the people who led him and Barb to where they are today. Neither of them ever expected the path their lives would take. But despite the difficulties, they had enjoyed building their lives in Haiti. It hadn't been a bed of roses for them, but they wouldn't trade it for anything.

As Dick reflected, he admitted he'd been scared of doing a lot of what he had done, but never to a point where he wanted to run away. The whole experience had been one obstacle after the next, and neither he nor Barb had realized how stressful it would all be. So many people depended on them—the volunteers, and the Haitian staff, and the Haitian patients. In some ways, they felt they had their lives in their hands—making sure the volunteers were safe, and trying to make sure the patients were getting the medical care they so desperately needed. It was difficult knowing that some of the patients were going to leave the clinic and go home, and not get better. But they knew they had to deal with the stress just like the Haitian people had to deal with stress and pain in their lives every day. And Dick dealt with his stress by learning to become a little bit Haitian—take things as they come and keep fighting to stay strong.

Of all the painful things Dick had seen over the years, one particular woman who came to the clinic had stuck in his mind. She had severe burns on her back from falling into a fire. Dick had seen hundreds of patients with burn wounds, but this woman's burns were particularly extensive—covering almost the full length of her back. Dick and the team were horrified by the severity of her injuries.

When it was time for the nurse to debride the woman's wound, Dick was in the exam room. He braced himself for the excruciating pain he knew the woman was about to feel. The nurse grabbed the top of the bandage and ripped it from the woman's back in a single, swift motion. Dick flinched, expecting to hear the young woman cry out in pain, but she never made a sound. Dick wasn't sure if her silence was because the wound had caused nerve damage or whether the woman was so accustomed to pain that a wound of that nature would no longer affect her. From what he had experienced thus far in Haiti in his life, Dick would wager that it was probably the latter.

Dick felt that the Haitians were tough in ways that was difficult for the American volunteers, including himself, to comprehend. Often, the medical team was the first to see a patient's burn wounds, even when they had occurred weeks earlier. Dick imagined these men, women, and children waiting for the team to arrive while coping with the types of injuries that would send any American to the emergency room immediately. He thought long and hard about this young woman—about the pain and fear her burns surely caused her—and yet it had been him who was the most frightened in the examining room.

Of all the lessons Dick learned in his decades in Haiti, the one that was most profound was that the things that would kill most people don't kill Haitians—they are just so strong they can

CHAPTER 12: DOUZ

survive. They are resilient in every part of their lives. Because of the conditions they live in, they have had to make the choice to survive. When it was either roll over and die, or survive, Haitians made up their minds to survive.

*

As Barb prepared for the arrival of each team to the clinic, one of her rituals was to write a quote on a small whiteboard in the kitchen for everyone to see. The quote was the same every time. Inevitably it would be erased between clinics and replaced with a grocery list, or something else, but she always made sure she wrote it up again for each newly arriving team. It came from the book *Mountains Beyond Mountains*, by Tracy Kidder. *Mountains Beyond Mountains* is a story about the life of Paul Farmer, the cofounder of the nonprofit organization Partners in Health. Paul Farmer has worked around the world providing health care to people in incredibly remote locations, including Haiti. The book gives detailed insight into the health care issues of not only Haitians, but many poor, neglected populations—those without access to doctors, or medicine, or resources, like clean water, to live healthy lives.

The quote is by Jim Yong Kim, Farmer's cofounder in Partners in Health, and a physician, as well as the current president of the World Bank. Kim worked closely with Paul Farmer in the earlier days of Partners in Health to offer low-cost treatment to patients in rural areas of Haiti. When questioned about their desire to treat the poorest patients in the world, Kim had responded, "They think we're unrealistic. They don't know we're crazy."

When Barb read the book, and Kim's quote, she couldn't help smiling. She thought it perfectly captured with simplicity and humor the reasons she and Dick had built a clinic in Haiti, and why they decided to dedicate their lives to helping Haiti's poor and sick, even when it seemed foolish or impossible to do so. She proudly wrote it on the board, along with Kim's name, and reference to the book it was quoted from.

In early 2011, a nurse named Diane was volunteering at the clinic. She was from New Hampshire, and she had worked at Dartmouth-Hitchcock Medical Center at the same time that Jim Yong Kim was the president of Dartmouth College. While in Haiti, Diane took a picture of the quote written on the whiteboard. When she got home, she sent a letter to Kim along with the photo, as well as other pictures of the clinic. Shortly after, Kim responded with a letter of his own.

Dear Diane,

Thank you so much for your generous service to those in need through the Friends of the Children of Haiti. I also appreciate the photos you sent. I'd much rather have my words written on a white board in the kitchen of a clinic in Cyvadier than on a bronze plaque anywhere else.

Warmly,
Jim Yong Kim

*

The morning after my arrival, I woke up early, despite the fact that Dick, Barb, and I had stayed up late talking. Although we had been alone the night before, this morning was the first time I realized how different it was to be at the clinic without the team, or the Haitian staff or patients. By 8:00 a.m., the clinic normally

CHAPTER 12: DOUZ

would have been in full swing. Some patients, entering the gates before 7:00 a.m., would have already seen a doctor and been to the pharmacy. As I lay in bed, instead of hearing people milling about outside the clinic, everything was quiet, and calm.

I went downstairs to the kitchen. Dick and Barb were already up, sitting at one of the plastic tables, reading. I joined them. Barb mentioned that in a few days, right after I was scheduled to leave, Martin and his wife would be bringing their kids to the clinic to visit. It would be the grandchildren's first time in Haiti, and Barb was excited that they would have a chance to see what their grandparents did and understand a little more about why she and Dick had missed birthdays and other family gatherings in years past.

Over a breakfast of fruit and toast, we continued our conversation from the night before. Dick explained how nothing happens quickly in Haiti, and sometimes it seems like nothing ever changes. Many times it didn't seem like they were making a dent at all, no matter how hard they worked. But at some point, over the years, they honestly began to feel as though they saw a difference in the health of the people that came to the clinic, and that was so important for them both. They had spent a long time trying to make change, and now, as they both approached eighty years old, they felt confident that they had helped Haitians receive consistent medical care, as well as given them hope for their futures.

We continued to talk throughout the day, moving to the patio after breakfast, then back to the kitchen for lunch, and back once more to the patio in the early afternoon to take in the view. That was about as much as Dick and Barb did during the day—they weren't moving fast anymore, but they still loved being in Haiti as much as they could be, both with the team, and with the

Haitians, who were so dear to them. And it didn't matter if they were moving slow. Whether Dick was running or not, he was still getting up the stairs of the clinic.

Boyer arrived just before dinner, knowing I was eager to get a chance to talk to him. After we ate, Dick suggested that Boyer take me somewhere, figuring it would give me a chance to see something new in Jacmel, as well as get out of the clinic for at least a small part of the day.

Boyer and I got into the truck and headed down the road out of the clinic gates. The truck slowly bounced down the gravel path, as we passed Esperidon's house and the small shelter where patients wait to get into the clinic. As we got to the end of the road, and turned onto the main highway, we passed Son Son's on the corner. As I looked out the window, my eyes followed the path that Dick had walked many times with volunteers and friends—Paul, Jean Michel, Belony, Boyer, Nelson, and Garron. We passed houses, and hotels, and lottery huts. We passed by the entrance to the Hotel Cyvadier. We passed by the Sea of Love. We drove past Ti Mioullage Beach. The air was cool, and the breeze felt refreshing on my face.

When we arrived at our destination, the Cap Lamandou Hotel, we ordered scotch from the bar and walked down to the pool to find a table. Almost no one else was at the hotel, but Boyer still knew the only other couple on the patio and politely chatted in Creole with them for a moment as I sifted through my notes. When he sat down a few minutes later, we started talking, first about Boyer's work at the clinic and then about what he thought the clinic meant to the Haitian people. About forty-five minutes into our conversation, I asked Boyer what the thought Haitian people wanted out of life. "What do the Haitian people want?" he repeated back to me, taking a second, and a sip off his drink,

CHAPTER 12: DOUZ

to consider his answer.

"Haitian people want electricity twenty-four hours a day. They want security, they want to see some progress in the country—they want to see something happening. They want paved roads, and industry. They want jobs. They want to see tourism come to the country."

We talked at length about the issue of security. Boyer explained that although security in Haiti was better today than it was even two or three years ago, crime could still be a problem at times. He shared a story, from not too long before, about people in Jacmel setting up roadblocks because of a missing transformer. EDH had installed one in a particular zone of Jacmel. The Haitians there were ecstatic to have a consistent supply of electricity, and for some people it was the first time they had ever had power in their homes. But a few months later, it suddenly disappeared. No one could seem to get any answers from EDH or the police about the missing transformer, and the Haitians grew aggravated and once again created a roadblock and set it on fire. When the police showed up, a fight ensued as both sides argued and threw rocks at one another. It went on for several hours before a local politician intervened and promised to buy a new transformer to replace the missing one just to end the dispute.

"Can you blame the Haitians for getting upset? All they wanted was electricity so they could live better," Boyer said to me.

Despite the tense story, Boyer didn't feel that Haiti was an unsafe country to travel to. He passionately urged for a push in tourism, wanting foreigners to see for themselves the beauty of the country. From its arts and culture, to its beaches, to Carnival, he explained, Haiti is a paradise that has much to offer people around the world.

He paused. He seemed satisfied with his answer, so I asked him my next question—Can Haiti sustain on its own?

Boyer's face lit up. He answered my question with a proverb, a common custom in Haiti. "The men around the power are not the men in power."

Boyer elaborated on the abuse of power in Haiti. He explained that it is difficult to change the system and how power is managed so that the country can sustain itself. Haiti is a country where the people that come into power don't like the country as much as they like themselves, he continued. He believed that other countries that used to help Haiti for years and years weren't seeing any changes in the power, or in Haiti, and he feared that they were growing tired of helping.

"But we still need help. We need a lot of help."

*

Dick and Barb Hammond have attended every clinic that their lives have allowed. Through natural disasters, and security issues, and serious health concerns, nothing could keep them away, and no one could convince them that they shouldn't go back. But there will be a time when they physically can't travel to Haiti anymore. They know the volunteers and Haitian staff can, and will, continue without them, and the Haitian patients will still be able to rely on the clinic in their lives.

It is Dick and Barb's dream to see the FOTCOH clinic open year-round. They would like the volunteer teams to continue to visit the clinic on a regular schedule, but they want to see the clinic run by Haitian medical staff for the remainder of the year. They don't know whether this dream will ever be obtained, especially for Dick and Barb to see in their lifetimes. As

CHAPTER 12: DOUZ

always, funding is the main concern—having the money to buy medications, pay Haitian staff, and keep the clinic maintained. But Dick and Barb are hopeful. They know the clinic is too important not to go on, and they are confident that it will continue to grow long after they are gone.

Whenever there was a team in Haiti working at the clinic, Dick always took the time to stroll out to the front of the property at least once a day. In between writing receipts, and making phone calls, he made a point to step away from his desk and greet the Haitian patients, even when it started to become taxing for him to make the long walk outside. But he wouldn't miss getting a chance to say "Bonswa" to the Haitians, whether he knew them personally or not. Although, every Haitian who came to clinic already knew who Dick and Barb were, even if they hadn't met them—they had been told what they had done for Jacmel and for Haiti, and what they had done for the Haitian people.

One afternoon, Dick walked out to the clinic gates to see how big the crowd was on that particular day. After standing around for a few minutes and greeting the staff and the patients, he turned around to head back to the clinic. An older Haitian woman was walking down the path towards Dick on her way out of the clinic, her medication bag from the pharmacy hanging off her wrist. When she got within a few feet of him, she raised her arms and put her hands up in the air, and said, "Mèsi, Papa! Mèsi, Papa! Thank you, Father! Thank you, Father!" as she looked up to the sky. Dick could see that she was thanking God for her day, for allowing her to make it to the clinic to receive care. Dick responded to her motions, and words by repeating her praise as he looked up at the sky, raising his arms in the same manner, waving his hands in the air. "Wi, Mèsi, Papa! Wi, Mèsi, Papa! Yes, Thank you, Father! Yes, Thank you, Father!" he said just as grandly as the woman had. But then, the woman suddenly stopped walking, right in front of Dick, and sternly said, "No! MÈSI, PAPA!" this time with her arms held out directly in front of her as she looked into Dick's eyes. It was then that he realized she was thanking him. Dick looked at her, not knowing how to respond. She seemed satisfied that Dick understood her clearly, and she continued down the path. Dick too returned to his walk, heading back to the clinic, and as he did, he looked up to the sky, and with a whole new feeling to the words, again said, "Mèsi, Papa."

fen a

EPILOGUE

Dick and Barb's children live in various cities around the United States. Melissa is living in Bellevue, Illinois. Matthew is retired from the US Navy and living in Washington state. He currently works for Boeing. Martin is living in Missouri and working in management for Stratmann Co. Michelle lives and works in Wisconsin. William passed away on August 6, 2012. Harry Hosey died in 2000. Alice Hosey passed away in 2001. Theresa Patterson still runs the Twinning Parish Program out of Nashville, Tennessee. Father Donice Redori works in a parish in South Florida. Father LaBourne retired to France, where he passed away in 2015. William Penn is a priest in Little Haiti in Miami. Belony passed away in 2009. Esperidon passed away in 2014. His son, Louinel, remains as the groundskeeper for the clinic and still lives in the house on the property. Jean Michel lives and works in Jacmel. Dick still speaks with him from time to time. Natasha is living and working in Jacmel. Milo is in the Dominican Republic in medical school. Gerald received a degree in civil engineering, and he is currently looking for a job in Port-au-Prince. Boyer continues to work as the Haitian director of FOTCOH. He is also pursuing a law degree. Nelson continues to work in his practice at the Dr. Martinez Hospital. He is the Haitian medical director for FOTCOH and works closely with Garron in the surgery program. Nelson's wife, Anne, gave birth to a healthy boy in France. They named him Mickael. The family returned to Jacmel in time for Cardelina to attend school in September 2010. They recently had another son, Sebastian.

Garron Lukas continues to work as the director of the surgical program for FOTCOH. He travels to Haiti four times a year to perform surgery. His wife Sharon still works as a nurse. They live in South Carolina.

St. Anthony's Church supported St. Dominic's Parish until 2012 through the PTPA.

*

Dick and Barb were at the clinic in July 2015 knowing it could very well be the last time they would visit Haiti together. At the time, they were both seventy-eight years old. Barb has not been back since, but Dick continues to travel to Haiti a few times a year—most recently with the July 2016 medical team.

Dick and Barb still travel extensively throughout the United States to visit family and friends all over the country. In April 2016, Dick and Barb visited their fiftieth state in the United States. They went on a cruise to Hawaii.

Dick and Barb Hammond would like to thank their family, their friends, and all the FOTCOH volunteers. Without the support of so many people, Friends of the Children of Haiti would not exist.

———

To find out more about Friends of the Children of Haiti, or learn how you can donate or volunteer, visit:

www.fotcoh.org

Author Acknowledgements

I would like to thank Dick and Barb Hammond for sharing their stories and for their hospitality, both in Haiti and at their home in Ft. Lauderdale. I would also like to thank my family for their support. Thanks to Andre Boyer, Frantzso Nelson, Garron Lukas, Theresa Patterson, Kevin Hosey, Beth Kramer, Diane Bilotta, and Larry Shank for their stories and interviews. I would like to thank all the FOTCOH volunteers for the opportunity to share their stories from the blog *Voices from the Clinic*—without you taking your time to work in Haiti and share your experiences, these wonderful stories could not be told.

I would like to thank Erin Briggs for reading my first unreadable draft and offering invaluable suggestions. Justin Briggs for reading a more readable draft. Ward Tefft for his support and direction. Valley Haggard for her recommendations. Liza Kate Boisineau for being the dearest of friends and her willingness to not only read multiple drafts, but to discuss this project with me endlessly. My editor Elizabeth Ferris for her expertise and encouragement, and to Spencer Hansen and Christina Gleixner, I can't say enough about your involvement in getting this book completed.

And to Jim, who is the hardest working person I know—thank you for never giving up on anything in life.

ABOUT THE AUTHOR

Shelley Briggs Callahan has traveled extensively across the United States and around the world reporting on the burden of poverty and working to support communities in need. From digging wells in Colombia, managing medical teams in Haiti, and reporting on the slums in Kenya and Ethiopia, Callahan has steadfastly committed herself to supporting the underprivileged.

The House of Life is her first book. You can read more of her work at shelleybriggscallahan.com.

BIBLIOGRAPHY

"2010 Jacmel Earthquake," *Wikipedia*, last modified July 21, 2016, http://enwikipedia.org/wiki/2010_Earthquake_in_Jacmel.

Alan, Greg. "Haiti's Cultural Capital Jacmel Damaged In Quake," *National Public Radio*, January 20, 2010, http://www.npr.org/templates/story/story.php?storyId=122755202.

Beaubien, Jason. "What happened to the aid meant to rebuild Haiti?," *National Public Radio*, February 28, 2013, http://www.npr.org/sections/healthshots/2013/02/28/172875646/what-happened-to-the-aid-meant-to-rebuild-haiti.

"Between Friends: News from Friends of the Children of Haiti; Friends begins surgical program," *Friends of the Children of Haiti Newsletter*, October 2007.

Bhatia, Pooja. "A Symbol of Hope for Haiti, a Landmark Again Stands Tall," *New York Times*, January 10, 2011, from http://www.nytimes.com/2011/01/11/world/americas/11haiti.html.

Burt, Al, and Bernard Diedrich. *Papa Doc & The Tonton Macoutes*. Princeton, NJ: Markus Weiner Publishers, 2005.

Carroll, Rory. "Haiti: Mud cakes become staple diet as cost of food soars beyond a family's reach," *The Guardian*, July 28, 2008, http://www.theguardian.com/world/2008/jul/29/food.internationalaidanddevelopment.

Collier, Paul. Haiti: *From Natural Catastrophe to Economic Security*. Department of Economics, Oxford University, January 2009.

Connor, Tracy, Hannah Rappleye, and Erika Angulo. "What does Haiti Have to Show for $13 Billion in Earthquake Aid?," *NBC News*, January 12, 2015, http://www.nbc news.com/news/investigations/what-does-haiti-have-show-13-billion-earthquake-aid-n28166.

Daniticat, Edwidge. *After the Dance*. New York: Crown Journeys, 2002.

Diaz, Junot. "Apocalypse: What Disasters Reveal," *Boston Review*, May 1, 2011, http://www. bostonreview.net/junot-diaz-apocalypse-haiti-earthquake.

Dubois, Laurent. *Haiti: The Aftershocks of History*. New York: Picador, 2012.

Farmer, Paul. *Aids & Accusation: Haiti and the Geography of Blame.* Berkeley: University of California Press, 1992.

———. *Haiti: After the Earthquake.* New York: Public Affairs, 2011.

———. *The Uses of Haiti.* Monroe, ME: Common Courage Press, 2006.

Friends of the Children of Haiti. *FOTCOH Medical Guidelines.* Peoria, IL: October 2002, revised December 2012.

Freeman, Bryant C. *Third-World Folk Beliefs and Practices: Haitian Medical Anthropology.* Institute of Haitian Studies, University of Kansas, La Presse Evangelique, 2007.

Fuller, Alexandra. "Haiti on Its Own Terms." *National Geographic Magazine,* December 2016, 99–119.

Girard, Phillippe. *Haiti: The Tumultuous History - From Pearl of the Caribbean to Broken Nation.* New York: Palgrave Macmillan, 2010.

Griffin, Michael, and Jennnie Weiss Block, eds. *In the Company of the Poor: Conversations with Dr. Paul Farmer and Fr. Gustavo Gutierrez.* Maryknoll, NY: Orbiz Books, 2013.

Guides Panorama Haiti: Jacmel & Le Sud-Est. Montreal: Les Imprimeries Transcontinental, 2003.

"Haiti Earthquake Facts and Figures," *Disaster Emergency Committee,* retrieved June 26, 2016 from http://www.dec.org.uk/articles/haiti-earthquake-facts-and-figures.

"Haiti Earthquake Fast Facts," *CNN Library,* December 13, 2015, http://www.cnn.com/2013/12/12/world/haiti-earthquake-fast-facts.

"History," *Parish Twinning Program of the Americas,* http://www.parishprogram.org/history.

"Hôtel Montana," *Wikipedia,* last modified April 21, 2016, http://en.wikipedia.org/wiki/Hotel_Montana.

"Jacmel," *Wikipedia,* last modified July 2, 2016, http://en.wikipedia.org/wiki/Jacmel.

Katz, Jonathan M. *The Big Truck That Went By: How the World Came to Save Haiti and Left Behind a Disaster.* New York: Palgrave Macmillan, 2013.

Kristof, Nicholas. "A Girl's Escape," Opinion Page, *New York Times,* January

1, 2014, http://www.nytimes.com/2014/02/opinion/kristof-a-girls-escape. html.

Laurent, Oliver. "Haiti Earthquake: Five Years After," *Time*, January 12, 2015, http://time.com/3662225/haiti-earthquake-five-year-after/.

Lonely Planet Travel Guide: Dominican Republic & Haiti. Victoria: Lonely Planet Publications, 2002.

Luciano, Phil. "Friends Saving Lives in Haiti," *Peoria Magazine*, December 2010, http://www.peoriamagazine.com/ibi/2010/dec/friend-saving-lives-haiti.

Marshall, Mariene. "Haiti: Throwing Good Money after Bad?," *BBC World Service*, audio blog post, August 2015, http://www.bbc.co.uk/programmes p02ybvlr?ocid=social flow_facebook.

Ramachandran, Vijaya, and Julie Walz. "Haiti's earthquake generated a $9bn response—Where did the money go?," *The Guardian*, January 14, 2013, https://www.theguardian.com/global-development/poverty-matters/2013/jan/14/haiti-earthquake-where-did-money-go.

Schacochis, Bob. *The Immaculate Invasion*. New York: Grove Press, 1999.

Schuller, Mark. "Haiti's Food Riots," *International Socialist Review* 59 (May–June 2008), retrieved August 28, 2016 from http://isreview.org/issues/59/rep-haiti.shtml.

Schuller, Mark. *Killing with Kindness: Haiti, International Aid, and NGOs*. Published by Author, 2012.

Simons, Marlise. "For Haiti's Tourism, the Stigma of AIDS is Fatal," *New York Times*, November 29, 1983, retrieved February 8, 2014 from http://www.nytimes.com /1983/11/29/world/for-haiti-s-tourism-the-stigma-of-aids-is-fatal.html.

"The Canadian Red Cross Lays the Cornerstone at the Saint-Michele Hospital in Jacmel," news release, *The Canadian Red Cross*, December 10, 2013, http://www.redcross.ca/ about-us/newsroom-/news-releases/latest-news/the-canadian-red-cross-lays-the-cornerstone-at-the-saint-michel-hospital-in-jacmel.

"Venezuela's Continuing Aid to Haiti." Press Office of the Embassy of the Bolivian Republic of Venezuela to the United States, January 2013, http://www.embavenez-us.org/factsheet/01272010-venezuelasaidtohaiti.pdf.

"Voices from the Clinic," *FOTCOH Blog*, https://fotcoh.wordpress.com.

Wilentz, Amy. *The Rainy Season*. New York: Simon & Schuster, 1989.

Wucker, Michele. *Why the Cocks Fight: Dominicans, Haitians, and the Struggle for Hispaniola*. New York: Hill and Wang, 1999.